D1549606

Wellington
at war

Wellington
at war

Chaz Bowyer

LONDON
IAN ALLAN LTD

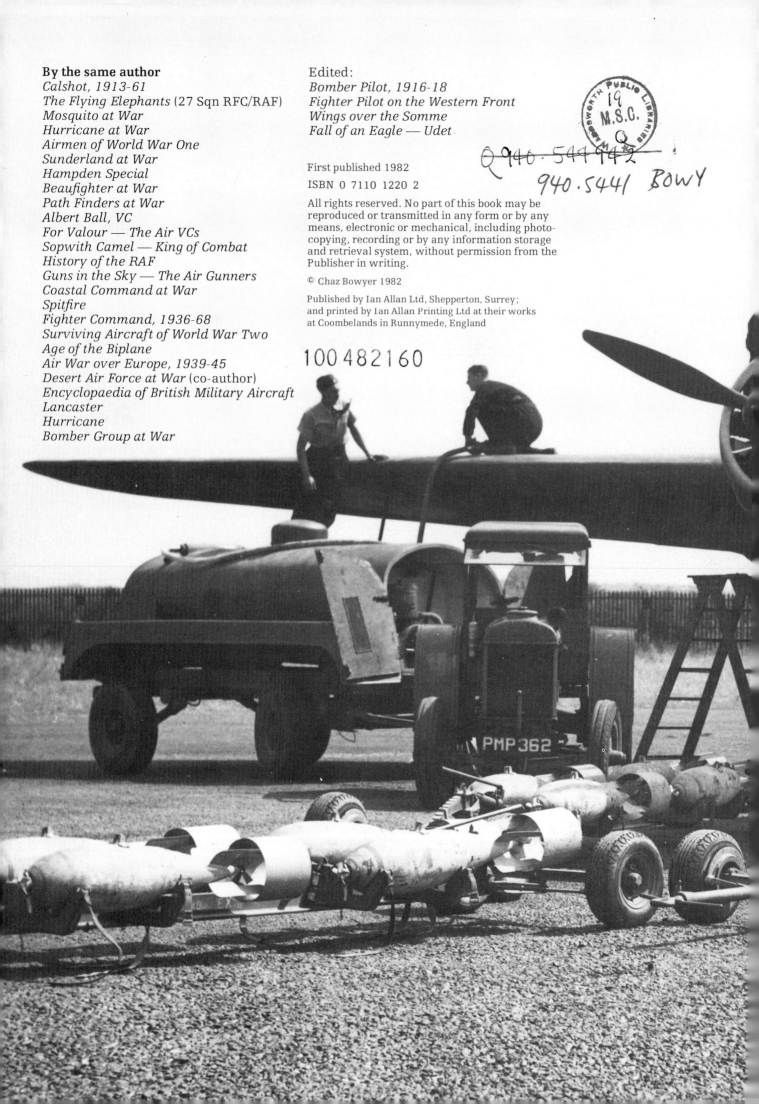

By the same author
Calshot, 1913-61
The Flying Elephants (27 Sqn RFC/RAF)
Mosquito at War
Hurricane at War
Airmen of World War One
Sunderland at War
Hampden Special
Beaufighter at War
Path Finders at War
Albert Ball, VC
For Valour — The Air VCs
Sopwith Camel — King of Combat
History of the RAF
Guns in the Sky — The Air Gunners
Coastal Command at War
Spitfire
Fighter Command, 1936-68
Surviving Aircraft of World War Two
Age of the Biplane
Air War over Europe, 1939-45
Desert Air Force at War (co-author)
Encyclopaedia of British Military Aircraft
Lancaster
Hurricane
Bomber Group at War

Edited:
Bomber Pilot, 1916-18
Fighter Pilot on the Western Front
Wings over the Somme
Fall of an Eagle — Udet

First published 1982
ISBN 0 7110 1220 2

© Chaz Bowyer 1982

Published by Ian Allan Ltd, Shepperton, Surrey;
and printed by Ian Allan Printing Ltd at their works
at Coombelands in Runnymede, England

Contents

Cover: Wellington III, Z1572, VR-Q, of No 419 ('Moose') Sqn, RCAF, circa May 1942.
C. E. Brown

Title page: In Indian skies. Two of 99 Sqn's Wellingtons in the 'Forgotten War' zone, 1944.
IWM

Left: Trolley train of 250lb GP bombs waiting for loading to a 149 Sqn Wellington at Mildenhall, while refuelling is completed.

Introduction

Any student of the RAF's bomber effort during 1939-45 can be forgiven if, after reading the wealth of literature published since then, he/she reaches the conclusion that the vast bulk of that effort was undertaken by Lancasters, Halifaxes, and/or Mosquitos. No one could deny the superb contributions made by all those aircraft, yet it is too often forgotten that until any of those designs appeared on the operational scene in significant numbers, ie until well into 1942, the full responsibility for carrying the air offensive into German skies was undertaken by several pre-1939 designs of twin-engined bombers. These included the Blenheim, Hampden, Whitley, and — especially — a design which was destined to remain in first-line operational service throughout the war and, incidentally, be built in greater quantities than *any* other RAF bomber during those years — the Vickers Wellington.

Universally nicknamed 'Wimpy' after the hamburger-gulping trencher-man J. Wellington Wimpy in the prewar Popeye strip cartoon series, the ubiquitous Wellington ultimately undertook every role and duty possible for an aircraft of its configuration. Primarily a bomber, it became equally effective as a submarine hunter-killer, torpedo-strike weapon, reconnaissance vehicle, freight-wagon and supply-dropper, VIP transporter, all-round trainer, ambulance, and general communications hack. Its strength of construction became a byword in aircrew circles, and many hundreds of crews owe their lives to the Wimpy's ability to absorb frightening battle damage and still 'bring 'em back alive'. In effect, the Wellington was almost the last of the RAF's 'cloth-bombers' — metal-constructed with fabric skinning — yet most ex-Wimpy crews would swear that it was the greatest such design.

The Wellington's origin can be traced to an Air Ministry Specification, B.9/32, issued to tender on 20 October 1932, for a new, twin-engined, monoplane, medium bomber for the RAF; a specification which also 'gave birth' to the Handley Page Hampden and Harrow bombers. With amendments and modifications in subsequent years, mainly for greater weight parameters and increased power, this AM Spec eventually spawned the Vickers B.9/32 prototype, serialled K4049. It made its first flight on 15 June 1936 at Brooklands, and in the same month it was proposed to call the new design Crecy, though this title was changed to Wellington three months later. K4049 commenced its flight trials and immediately displayed excellent potential, resulting in the issue of AM Spec 29/36 in February

1937 for a redesigned production version, the Mk 1 Wellington, for Service use. Before completion of its flight testing, however, K4049 was totally destroyed in a flying trial on 19 April 1937, breaking up in mid-air. In its Mk 1 production configuration the Wellington incorporated many necessary Service requirements and additions, including enclosed, power-operated gun turrets in the nose, belly and tail positions, bomb bay installation, *et al*; the first production example, L4212, making its first flight on 23 December 1937, fitted with two Bristol Pegasus XX engines.

The first RAF unit to commence re-equipment with Wellingtons was No 99 Squadron, based at Mildenhall, Suffolk, which received its first example, L4215, on 10 October 1938. Nine more squadrons began re-equipment before the outbreak of war — Nos 38, 149, 9, 148, 115, 37, 75, 214, 215 in chronological sequence. Thus, in September 1939, eight Wellington squadrons comprised the total strength of No 3 Group, Bomber Command, while the remaining pair (Nos 75 and 148) were Group Pool units with No 6 Group. By May 1945 a total of 73 Squadrons and a myriad of training or other specialised Flights or units were to have flown Wellingtons in some guise. Production of Wellingtons commenced in 1937 and was to continue until October 1945, during which period 11,460 production Wellingtons were built — the greatest number of *any* British bomber *ever* produced. The Wellington remained in RAF service after the war — mainly Mk X variants flown as trainers or airborne classrooms — until the type's ultimate retirement from RAF livery in late March 1953. Only one solitary example of a complete Wellington now exists; MF628, a Mk X built in 1944, which, after a chequered career, was finally handed over to the RAF Museum, Hendon, on 26 October 1971, where it may be viewed today in splendidly refurbished state.

The history of the Wellington has yet to be recorded in fully comprehensive form, and I would emphasise immediately that this volume is in no way intended to masquerade as any such 'biography' of that superb old lady. Its theme — as in all titles in this particular series — is simply a sincere evocation of the Wimpy, of the type of men and women who flew or tended her and, I hope, an authentic recreation of contemporary 'atmosphere' of the Wellington's hey-day. Towards that purpose I have been helped by the extraordinary generosity of many, many ex-air and ground crews who served with Wimpys during the years 1938-45; all of whom volunteered accounts, anecdotes, information, and the loan of precious photographs and documents. The list is long, and therefore detailed as a separate appendix in the rear of this book. In addition I received totally selfless and immediate practical help from a number of friends and colleagues. Of these I would mention particularly R. C. B. 'Chris' Ashworth, Roy Bonser, Jim Crowshaw, Sid Finn, E. 'Ted' Hine of the Imperial War Museum Photo Library, Phil Jarrett, Eric Morgan, Ken Munson, Bryan Philpott, Bart Rijnhout, Bruce Robertson, Ray Sturtivant, and G. S. 'Stu' Leslie. And no book of mine can fail to illustrate the skill and expertise of Dave Gray of Walkers Studios, Scarborough, who constantly produces splendid reproductions of faded and ancient photographs for use in illustration. To each of those mentioned I offer an open hand of sincere gratitude.

Chaz Bowyer
Norwich, 1982

Below: Wellington LN323 sets off to bomb a target in Italy, 1944. *IWM*

Roots

Above: Father-Figure. The first Wellington prototype, K4049, in its original configuration, June 1936. Engines are 915hp Pegasus Xs. *Vickers Ltd*

Left: K4049 being trundled over the River Wey toll-bridge at Brooklands. All aircraft bearing RAF roundels were not required to have the toll charged . . . *Vickers Ltd*

Above: L4212, the prototype Wimpy Mk 1, taking off from Brooklands on its first flight, 23 December 1937, piloted by Mutt Summers. *Vickers Ltd*

Right: Barnes Wallis's geodetic design illustrated by these Mk 1 Wimpy fuselages in the Weybridge erecting shop, 1939. *Vickers Ltd*

Above left: Close-up of the 'basket-weave' construction; an internal view from the nose position, with pilot's position in foreground. *Vickers Ltd*

Above: L4250, the prototype Wellington Mk II at Brooklands, fitted with Rolls-Royce Merlin Xs, which made its first flight on 3 March 1939. Later used for experimental 40mm cannon trials, L4250 ultimately became a training airframe (3477M) in December 1942. *Vickers Ltd*

Left: L4251, the prototype Mk III Wimpy, which first flew on 19 May 1939. Engines were Hercules HEISM two-stage supercharger units. *Vickers Ltd*

Right: P9238, a Mk 1c converted to become the Mk III production model, with improved Hercules engines. The Mk III Wimpy became a prime strike aircraft for Bomber Command from 1941. *Vickers Ltd*

Below: R1220, the Mk IV prototype, viewed just after roll-out from the Chester factory, late 1940. Engines were 1,050hp Pratt & Whitney Twin Wasps. First RAF deliveries of production examples began in June 1941. *Vickers Ltd*

Above: L4250, the prototype Mk II, fitted experimentally with a 40mm Vickers cannon mid-upper turret, and twin fin/rudders, January 1942.
Vickers Ltd

Right: The same machine, with 40mm cannon installation, but with normal, single fin/rudder, and rear gun turret location faired over.
Vickers Ltd

Below: Postwar view of a Wellington T10 trainer, NC425, of No 7 Air Navigation School (ANS), 1948. Note retention of front and rear gun turrets here.
Sqn Ldr D. J. Munro via R. Bonser

Above: Shark-nose. Wellington Mk VI, DR484, fitted with RR Merlin 60 engines and Type 423 bomb gear. Designed for high altitude bombing, with a pressure cabin housing entire crew of four. This particular machine was eventually reduced to spares on 21 December 1942.
Vickers Ltd

Above: A Wellington B10 of No 1689 Flight.
via R. C. B. Ashworth

Right: Hybrid. Wellington II, Z8570, fitted with Merlin 62 main engines, and a tail-installation of a Whittle jet engine, at Bruntingthorpe, 1944

Below: Wellington LN175, a Mk X modified for testing Rolls-Royce Dart turbo-props later used in the Vickers Viscount et al. *Vickers Ltd*

Right: Last of the Breed. Wellington X, MF628, the sole surviving complete Wimpy in the world. Built in 1944, it was ultimately handed over to the RAF Museum, Hendon on 26 October 1971, where, in splendidly refurbished state, it may be viewed today.
Vickers Ltd

In the Beginning

Flying Officer (later, Group Captain) A. Montagu-Smith was the 99 Squadron adjutant when he flew a Wellington for the first time on 8 November 1938. His account of his personal reactions and experiences during those early days probably mirror most contemporary pilots' views of the first Wimpys:

'With the introduction of the Wellington into RAF squadron service in the autumn of 1938 a whole new era of military flying began for the pilots of Bomber Command. Until then the night bomber force consisted mainly of squadrons equipped with the Handley Page Heyford; a 100mph biplane with open cockpit, fixed undercarriage, and simple instrument panel — in fact, merely a refinement of the bombers used in France towards the end of World War 1. The Wellington was something entirely new.

'To the pilots of No 99 Squadron at Mildenhall, Suffolk, who were the first to receive the type, the changeover was exciting. Squadron pilots collected the first aircraft from Weybridge in October 1938, and caused some concern by arriving back at Mildenhall after dark, thus necessitating night landings. As one of the first officers to fly a squadron Wellington — L4220 on 8 November 1938 — I found it to be an exhilarating occasion, albeit somewhat claustrophobic due to the unfamiliar enclosed cockpit. Handling the aircraft required a very different technique from that of the Heyford. For the first time one had to operate a retractable undercarriage — which could easily be

Below: Wimpy crew about to board their aircraft, July 1940.
Sport & General Agency

forgotten; flaps had to be used, while the full instrument panel was a source of wonderment. Until then one had relied upon the elementary turn-and-bank indicator; now an artificial horizon had to be got used to. In the Heyford the pilot sat high, on a level with the upper mainplane, but in the Wellington, with its short undercarriage, one seemed very near the ground.

'The final weeks of 1938 and first eight months of 1939 kept the pilots of 99 Squadron busy becoming efficient in operating the new aircraft, and in early 1939 the tempo of life at Mildenhall increased noticeably. The two resident squadrons, Nos 99 and 149, flew their Wellingtons by day and night continuously to achieve operational standards. For example, during April and May I carried out 35 various training sorties. On 25 May, during an exercise with the Fleet in the English Channel, flying L4297, I suffered a burst fuel pipe which necessitated a forced-landing at RAF Gosport. The consequent one-engine approach and landing was effected without difficulty, but it must be admitted that the let-down from 10,000ft with only one serviceable engine created a moment or two of distinct uneasiness. Gosport was more or less in a built-up area, and I knew that my approach with a heavily-laden aircraft had to be right first time — I could not go round again.

'In the summer of 1939 the Wellington squadrons were ordered to practise daylight, low-level flying, which seemed to indicate a possible change in the operational role. Anyway, it provided an excuse to indulge in "contour-chasing", and Wellingtons were to be seen low-flying all over Southern England. It was fun, but very tiring when kept up for a couple of hours or so. Then on 18 July 1939 an exercise of some magnitude was planned to begin. All the serviceable aircraft of No 3 Group, Bomber Command, led by the Air Officer Commanding (AOC), Air Commodore A. A. Thompson, set off from their respective bases in East Anglia for a formation "showing-the-

Top right: Sqn Ldr Montagu-Smith briefs his pilots of A Flt, 221 Sqn, at Bircham Newton, 1941. *C. Beaton/Air Ministry*

Right: Navigator's office in a 221 Sqn Wellington, Bircham Newton, 1941. *C. Beaton/Air Ministry*

Above: Peace Hazard. A 99 Sqn Wellington, bearing the unit's prewar codes VF, which had its tail fabric strip off in flight. Its pilot, Sgt Atkinson, was killed in action when serving with the Path Finder Force in later years.
S. C. Atkinson

Right: War Hazard. Tail damage to Wellington T2739 of 99 Sqn, after an encounter with a German nightfighter, early 1941. *PNA Ltd*

Below: Czech Threesome. Mk 1cs of 311 (Czech) Sqn, late 1940. Aircraft 'M' was R1410 which later served with 25 OTU and failed to return on 25/26 June 1942; 'K' was R1378 which crashed on 3 March 1942; while 'A' (T2541) also served as 'O-Orange' on 99 Sqn at one period.
Imperial War Museum

flag'' flight to France. However, bad weather south of London forced a change of plan, which was communicated to each aircraft of this very large formation by wireless — we did not have R/T. As a Flight Lieutenant now, I was leading a section of B Flight, 99 Squadron, in Wellington L4220. The result of this last-minute change of plan was chaotic. The new orders cancelled the French trip and substituted a tour along the south coast of England instead. As we flew west the weather got steadily worse, with low cloud and poor visibility, until it was difficult to even see the nearest aircraft ahead. Eventually I received a ''return to base'' signal from my wireless operator. At the same time, to my alarm, out of the gloom came a number of Wellingtons on a reciprocal course! These belonged to the leading squadrons returning home, having jumped the gun by following the leader before the signal had reached all aircraft. With Wellingtons gaily passing on either side of me, the scene can well be imagined — I can still remember the look of horror on the face of my second pilot-cum-navigator, Flg Off Hetherington, a New Zealander. However, we were able to extricate ourselves from this shambles, and miraculously there were no collisions.

'On 1 September 1939, in Wellington L4247, with the rest of 99 Squadron, I moved from Mildenhall to Newmarket Heath, which was to be our war station. During September and October training continued, although on a number of occasions the squadron ''bombed up'' and stood by for operations which were eventually scrubbed due to political reasons. Remember, at that period of the war bombing of the German mainland was forbidden. Thus, when 99 Squadron carried out its first sortie of World War 2 on 30 October, the target was the German Fleet reported somewhere in the Heligoland Bight. I took off in L4297 but bad weather on reaching the German coast prevented the squadron from sighting any enemy ships, and we recrossed the North Sea to Mildenhall after an uneventful flight. Much of the flight home was after nightfall and I can recall the problems of finding Mildenhall in a blacked-out countryside. All aircraft on this sortie had been ordered to land at Mildenhall for debriefing, but there was little control, if any, from the ground, with the result that there were numbers of

Wellingtons circling the Mildenhall district in the dark with pilots trying to identify the correct beacon.

'On 14 December 1939, No 99 Squadron set off on its second war sortie for the German coast with a full complement of 12 aircraft ie two flights of six — the normal size of a peacetime squadron. Strong opposition from enemy ships and aircraft was encountered and five Wellingtons and their crews were lost, while a sixth crashed on return, killing or injuring its crew members. This experience put 99 out of action for some time, while three squadron air gunners were recommended for and eventually awarded Distinguished Flying Medals.

In the winter of 1940 it was decided to form the first Wellington squadron for anti-submarine operations in Coastal Command, and on 21 November 1940 No 221 Squadron was reformed at Bircham Newton. In the following month I was posted to 221 Squadron and, as a Squadron Leader, was appointed commander of A Flight,

and because of my Wellington experience found myself as the unofficial squadron instructor. Our first aircraft were mainly cast-offs from bomber units for training and conversion use. Early in May 1941 the squadron became operational, and I flew to the new base at Limavady, Northern Ireland, on 2 May in Wellington W5671. We had by then received our new aircraft, fully equipped with ASV appendage including external antennae. All this extra equipment necessarily increased the overall weight of the aircraft considerably, and when carrying depth charges they felt very sluggish after take-off until speed had been built up.

'On 15 May 1941, flying in Wellington W5671, my crew and I located and attacked a U-boat well out in the Atlantic. This was 221 Squadron's first action, and (I believe) the first attack on an enemy submarine by a maritime Wellington in the war. It was an exhilarating moment for me as we dived in to the attack to release our

Top: Wellington Is, L4367 and L4369 of 75 Sqn during war exercises in August 1939. The white cross markings represented the 'Westland' ('friendly') forces of these war games.

Above: 75 Sqn Wimpys (L4367, nearest and L4370) at 12,000ft during the August 1939 war exercises.
Sport & General Agency

depth charges, which hit the water near the U-boat but not close enough to create any visible damage. However, morale received an excellent boost and the squadron felt that it was seriously 'in business'. There followed a period of intensive flying, with trips of nine and ten hours out over the Atlantic forming a regular pattern of life. All sorties were carried out at fairly low level, which meant ploughing through all sorts of unpleasant weather conditions, and we were usually pretty tired men after such long flights. On 10 June and again on 12 June 1941, my crew and I found boatloads of survivors from torpedoed merchant ships out in the Atlantic. These were heartrending scenes and we were gratified that on both occasions we were able to help rescue the unfortunate sailors by directing naval vessels to the relevant locations.

'By August 1941 the squadron had moved to St Eval, Cornwall, to help cover the Bay of Biscay, and on 5 August, in Wellington W5732 over the Bay, we attacked our second U-boat which was sighted on the surface. As we flew away after our attack we could see patches of oil and some pieces of wreckage floating on the sea. Although not sunk, we heard later that the submarine had been sufficiently damaged to force it to return to its base in France for repairs. We also received a congratulatory signal from the AOC, 19 Group. Our third attack on a U-boat came on 11 September 1941, again in the Bay of Biscay, but no positive results were seen.

'Two days later, on 13 September, in Wellington W5671, I flew my last sortie with 221 Squadron, and it proved to be very hectic. While on antisubmarine patrol well down in the Bay of Biscay we were intercepted by a Junkers Ju88 long-range fighter. As he closed in behind us for the attack I climbed at full throttle for cloud cover 2,000ft above. The Wellington responded well and we gained the safety of the overcast before the Ju88 pilot could get within lethal range. We all breathed a sigh of relief as I settled down for some ten minutes of instrument flying. When I let down below cloud and resumed my original course, with no Ju88 in sight, both engines of the Wellington stopped! The explanation was simple. In the excitement of avoiding the enemy fighter, we had forgotten to change over petrol tanks at the correct time. The effect on my crew was electric! I shouted, "Petrol cocks!" and there was a rush for the midway position in the aircraft. My second pilot had got there first and switched tanks. In the meantime, without any power, we were rapidly losing height and I was contemplating a ditching with a definite lack of enthusiasm. However, with less than 1,000ft to go both engines roared back to life again — the wonderful Wimpy had not let us down, and on completion of the patrol we returned to base to fly another day. In my own case, this was the end of my operational tour of duty with 221 Squadron. Sadly, after some 500 hours of Wimpy flying with Nos 99 and 221 Squadrons, I never flew a Wellington again.'

Above: L4304 of 148 Sqn in early 1939 livery. It later served with 75 Sqn, 15 OTU and 11 OTU before being struck off RAF charge on 19 November 1944.   *Crown copyright*

Right: No 149 Sqn's Wellingtons (nearest, L4272, LY-G) over Paris on 14 July 1939 (Bastille Day). An ex-9 Sqn machine, L4272 later became OJ-C with 149 Sqn, served with No 9 BATF and No 3 OTU, before becoming instructional airframe 2875M in December 1941.   *C. E. Brown*

Below: No 9 Sqn Wellingtons flying near Honington in early 1940, with ventral 'dustbin' gun turret extended under nearest aircraft N3000. This machine was later to see service with Nos 9, 40 adn 311 Sqns, then 12 OTU, 28 OTU, the Central Gunnery School (CGS) and the Air Transport Auxiliary (ATA), before being struck off RAF charge on 19 November 1944. *via T. Mason*

Early Days and Nights

Group Captain J. R. 'Benny' Goodman DFC, AFC completed 40 operational sorties in Wimpys during 1940-41 when, as a junior sergeant pilot, he commenced a lengthy and distinguished career. His account of just some of the varied facets of a Wimpy pilot's life during the first two years of the war give emphasis to the near-primitive conditions endured by the crews of Bomber Command then — and no less the courage and determination of those pioneering crews in the air offensive against Nazi Germany:

'I joined 37 Squadron — the "37th Foot" — at Feltwell, near Thetford, as a sergeant pilot in the middle of August 1940, when the Battle of Britain was at its height. Within a few days the squadron, indeed the whole of Bomber Command, was at instant readiness for operations against a German seaborne invasion, expected at any time. This meant that all personnel were confined to the station, and all aircraft were bombed up to maximum capacity with 18 250lb GP bombs. I was allocated as second dicky to the crew to Plt Off Herbert Ashton Clark, an ex-flight sergeant fitter who had turned pilot during the pre-war expansion of the Service. Not only was Nobby Clark very knowledgeable about what made aircraft tick, but he was also a first class pilot and navigator. If there is any one man to whom I have to be grateful for the fact that I survived two tours of ops in Bomber Command, that man is Nobby Clark. (He survived the war as a Wing Commander, DSO, DFC and became a farmer).

'Being on standby did not mean that we sat around waiting for the invasion fleet to set sail from Channel ports. In fact we hammered away at the German barges and also made regular sorties against targets in Germany. However, the squadron armourers were hard-pressed, because they were constantly bombing up or de-bombing aircraft. For example, an aircraft on standby, loaded with 18 250lb bombs, if it was detailed for normal operations, would need to be de-bombed and a mixed load of 500-pounders and incendiaries substituted. When it returned from its sortie, the aircraft would then again be loaded with 18 250lb bombs and resume its standby state.

'Our operational briefings covered three categories of target; the primary, the secondary, and something called SEMO or MOPA. The aim was to attack the primary if possible, but if for any reason this proved impossible — bad weather et al — then we were expected to go for the secondary, which would be similar in character though in a different area. If we could not find either of these targets then we would resort to SEMO or MOPA — meaning "Self-evident military objective" or "Military objective previously attacked". If no target in any of these categories could be found, then our strict orders were to bring the bombs back — remember, this was 1940; later in the war there was no such thing as bringing bombs back from Germany.

'One night be were briefed to attack the marshalling yards at Hamm, a favourite German target in those days. We duly arrived over the Ruhr but could not find Hamm, despite a good moon and diligent searching. The Ruhr smog was everywhere and also obscured the secondary target. After sculling around for a while at 3,000ft, we saw a train puffing along beneath us and we descended and identified it as a goods train. We decided this was a SEMO — indeed, it was a perfect target because it could neither stand and fight or run away. We made our bombing run straight along the railway line and dropped a stick of HE and incendiaries on the line of trucks, then turned away and flew well clear to await developments. These were not long in coming. Our incendiaries had

Right: No 37 Sqn Wellington crew, August 1940, Feltwell. From left: Unknown rear AG, Sgt J. R. Goodman (2/P), Plt Off H. A. Clark (Capt), Sgt W. W. W. Smith (Obs), Sgt 'Ginger' Jones (W/Op), and Sgt Ken Rutherford (AG, later killed in action). Note ice damage from props on fuselage fabric.
Grp Capt J. R. Goodman

Below: Wimpy T2888, 'R-Robert' of B Flt, 99 Sqn at Newmarket, November 1940 — the 'Jinx Kite' referred to in the text.
Grp Capt J. R. Goodman

Bottom: Crew of Wimpy T2888 'R-Robert', 99 Sqn, Newmarket, November 1940. From left: J. H. Parry (W/Op), J. R. Goodman (Capt), G. A. Masters (2/P), G. B. Cooper (Obs), R. Wickham (Front AG). *Grp Capt J. R. Goodman*

set some trucks on fire, while the HE had stopped the train. In seconds one of the trucks flared up, then an enormous explosion took place. Our Wimpy rocked as the blast hit her, so we scuttled away, undamaged, leaving behind a splendid firework display as what was clearly an ammunition train blew up.

'No pilot with any experience of Wellingtons would spin one intentionally, and no sane pilot would ever spin one at night. However, Nobby Clark and I found ourselves in the latter category soon after the ammunition train incident. We took off on the night of 5 October 1940 in our faithful T2508, ''T-Tommy'' and headed for the German barges crammed in the Rotterdam dock basins. We climbed steadily from Feltwell to 9,000ft and, after crossing the English coast at Southwold, tested all guns and headed for Holland. Eventually the front gunner uttered a laconic warning, ''Enemy coast ahead'' and we became especially watchful. The Hook of Holland loomed up out of the darkness and soon we could see Rotterdam and the target dock basins. The navigator now took his place in the nose and Nobby gently circled the town, then set ''T-Tommy'' straight at the docks. Meanwhile the Germans had not been idle; searchlights and flak were well in evidence. The heavy flak was something of a nuisance and from time to time there was a crump, crump as shells exploded

19

Above: R1333, the 'Broughton Bomber', which was initially delivered to 99 Sqn at Newmarket. Contrary to previous published statements this machine crashed, fully war-loaded, on take-off for an operational sortie on 18 December 1940, on the 'Devil's Dyke', and exploded in flames, killing the rear gunner.

Right: No 99 Sqn crew at Waterbeach, mid-1941. From left: L. B. 'Joe' Knight (F/AG), Bob Holden (2/P), Percy Hawkins (Wop/AG), F. G. 'Stan' Holloway (Capt), Jim Dermody (Obs, a New Zealander), and R. 'Bob' Butler (R/AG). All except Dermody were later to be killed on ops. *N. Didwell*

Below: Winter 1940-41 at Newmarket. A 99 Sqn Wimpy with appropriate protective covers in a snow landscape. *Planet News Ltd*

nearby. The bombing run continued and Nobby Clark concentrated on what was happening on the ground. I noticed our speed was dropping, then the bombs began to leave the racks as the navigator pressed the bomb release button. At this instant there was a loud bang as a shell exploded beneath us, and "T-Tommy" reared up like a startled horse, hovered momentarily, then fell over to starboard and rolled into a right-hand spin.

'When an aircraft spins the pilot is pressed hard into his seat by centrifugal force or reaction — call it what you will — and Nobby had his work cut out in applying left rudder and pushing the control column forward in his attempt to stop the spin. Nothing happened and the Wellington continued to flail downwards. I was pressed firmly against the metal former behind the pilots' cockpit and could barely move. Nobby now took emergency spin recovery action, blasting the throttles open and closed and moving the control column sharply back and forward in an attempt to shake the Wimpy out of its spin — "Tommy" merely continued to rotate. Nobby now called, "Jump, jump!", the order to abandon the aircraft. At this command I attempted to pull myself forward towards the nose in order to let the front gunner out of his turret, but I couldn't get forward. Looking again at the skipper, I could see that he was still trying to stop the spin, and I heaved myself across the bottom of the cockpit and grabbed the right rudder

pedal and pulled like mad. To my astonishment — and joy — it moved and helped Nobby to hold a little more left rudder. He blasted the engines again and the spin suddenly stopped, leaving us in a steep dive with all the blind-flying instruments haywire.

'Luckily, the night was clear with a good horizon, so we were able to level out and settle on to a good course until the instruments behaved normally, then we turned for home at about 1,000ft and limped along, gaining a little height as we progressed towards East Anglia. Nobby found that he could move the rudder but the elevators were stiff, so he decided to use the latter as little as possible. Some two hours later we arrived at Feltwell and Nobby brought "T-Tommy" in for a skilful landing, avoiding the use of flaps because their operation would also require considerable forward movement of the control column to hold the nose down. After landing the full extent of the damage was revealed. Large areas of fabric had been torn from the fuselage, but the major horror was that the elevators had moved bodily sideways and the rollers on which they rotated were just touching their companion rollers on the tailplane. We had been literally a fraction of an inch away from complete disaster.

'The time now came for me to take over a crew of my own, and I climbed aboard 37 Squadron's dual Mk 1c Wellington, R2937, with Nobby Clark's crew at their usual stations, but with

Above: Remarkably clear view
of interior of Wimpy T2888,
'R-Robert', 99 Sqn,
Newmarket, November 1940
— taken with a box Brownie
camera!
Grp Capt J. R. Goodman

Germany and they had not. However,
we quickly became friends and con-
ducted ourselves as a crew should, and
soon began to operate over Germany in
our own "Cloth Bomber" (as the
Wimpy was also known).

'My third trip as skipper was to be
Bremen and we bounced along the
flare path on the night of 16 October in
R3224 with everyone relaxed and the
Pegasus engines roaring reassuringly.
At 90mph I eased her gently into the
air — then things began to go wrong.
She absolutely refused to gain speed. I
checked that the wheels were up and
locked, then retracted the flaps which
had been set at 15 degrees before take-
off — the Wimpy accelerated to
95mph! I checked the cooling gills but
they were correctly set. The second
pilot and I went through everything
with a fine toothcomb but found
nothing to account for the aircraft's
strange behaviour. Meanwhile I'd
eased her gently upwards and levelled
out at 800ft with the exhaust rings
glowing red-hot. I throttled back
slightly and she began to lose height, so
back to full throttle we went. The most
urgent need now was to land as soon
as possible, but this could not be done
at once because aircraft of 37 and 75
(NZ) Squadrons were still taking off. So
round and round Feltwell we went
until at last I could fly over the take-off
point and flash my downward
indentification light and receive a
reassuring green from the airfield
control pilot's Aldis lamp, giving permission to land. The circuit and
approach to land were normal except
that a great deal of power had to be
used even though we were descending.
At last we crossed the airfield
boundary and levelled out above the
grass — there were no runways then. I
was a little too high so closed the
throttles — which was a mistake
because the Wimpy immediately sank
and landed heavily, driving the undercarriage through the wings. She
skidded along the ground quite gently
and came to a stop parallel to the flare
path. I switched off everything
electrical, there being a grave fire risk,
then the crew and I abandoned ship
smartly.

'We were met by the CO of 75
Squadron, who was OC Flying that
night, and I told him the strange story.
He said nothing and we walked round
the Wimpy together while he shone his
torch on the aircraft. When we were at
the trailing edge of the starboard wing

the squadron commander, Wg Cdr
"Willie" Merton (later, Air Chief
Marshal) in the right hand seat. I went
through all the drills under the CO's
eagle eye and put the Wimpy and its
crew through flight procedures which
were well-known and practised by us
all. After just over an hour the CO pro-
nounced himself satisfied and we
landed. I reported to this officer shortly
afterwards when he informed me that
I was now an aircraft captain! I was
just 19 years old, the youngest
"skipper" on the squadron! My chest
swelled with pride and I felt nine feet
tall — but I was soon to be cut down to
size. The thing I recall strongly about
my new crew is that every one of them
was older than me — two were even
married. The only advantage I had
over them was that I'd flown ops over

he suddenly stopped and said, "That's the trouble", pointing at the top of the wing at its deepest point. He was shining his torch at the petrol filler flaps, which I could see were down but not locked. These were metal hinged flaps covering the necks and caps of the main fuel tanks, and after refuelling these flaps had to be latched securely. Failure to do this would mean that on take-off these flaps would rise into the area of reduced air pressure above the wing and would become spoilers, destroying the smooth airflow over the wing and the precious lift it gave. This had happened to us — we might easily have been killed and no one would ever have known the cause. I should add that the airman responsible for not locking the filler flaps was given 28 days detention. No doubt he deserved this, but it was an object lesson to me and I became a positive misery about these flaps, particularly when I became an instructor at 15 OTU at the end of my ops tour; though I have little doubt that my insistence on checking they were locked saved other pilots' lives.

'Sadder and wiser now, in rapid succession I dropped visiting cards on Dusseldorf, Emden and Bremen, and then at the beginning of November No 37 Squadron become non-operational in order to prepare to fly out to the Middle East. We awaited the order to move, then quite suddenly I was struck down by a ghastly attack of 'flu and ended up in station sick quarters. Three days later the squadron flew off to Egypt, while I was eventually sent to another UK-based squadron in order to complete my tour; No 99 Squadron at Newmarket.

'My arrival at Newmarket could not have happened at a worse moment. The leading light on the squadron had failed to return from operations that night, and no one took much notice of the new arrival. Worse was to follow; I was allocated to B Flight and given the jinx aircraft, R-Robert, L7802. Every squadron had its jinx aircraft — one to which everything seemed to happen and which would go missing at the drop of a hat. In 99 Squadron there were two such kites — "B-Bertie" in A Flight, and "R-Robert" in B Flight. My arrival had coincided with the loss of the most experienced and popular captain in "B-Bertie". My new crew must have looked askance at me because they'd completed half a tour with "Ginger" Rothwell, a New Zea-

lander who had now gone on "rest" — if pounding a circuit at an OTU for up to 80 hours a month can be termed "rest". They did not relish the idea of changing skippers in mid-stream. Nor did I like the prospect of changing crews. In Bomber Command no one ever relished any change in crew; if, for example, a gunner was sick and was replaced by another for just one operation, the crew immediately become uneasy — in some odd way, they felt they had became more likely to get "the chop". However, the powers that be at HQ 3 Group had decided in their infinite wisdom that it made sense to post a Wellington skipper who'd completed half a tour to command a crew at another squadron who had also got through half a tour. In fact, it all worked out well and we

Top: Another 'inside' view of a Wellington, looking towards the nose. *IWM*

Above: Briefing, early 1941 style. *British Official*

finished our tour without too much bother — by contrast, my 37 Squadron crew ultimately perished in the Middle East.

'I lost no time in telling my new crew that I didn't believe in jinx aircraft, and that I had certainly no intention of going down in "R-Robert". Brave words, and oddly prophetic; we bore charmed lives in "R-Robert", but on the two occasions on which we went on leave "R-Robert" went down with other crews, so the jinx was preserved. Nor did "B-Bertie" fare any better. Aircraft workers at the Broughton factory at Chester "bought" a Wellington, R1333, and "presented" it to Bomber Command, where it was allocated to A Flight, 99 Squadron. It was given the code letter "B", possibly because it was named "The Broughton Bomber", and prepared for operations. The day came when this "B-Bertie" became operational and a delegation from the works came to watch the take-off. She got airborne and almost immediately crashed into the Devil's Dyke at Newmarket, catching fire and then exploding with the loss of all on board.

'The winter 1940-41 was as cold as charity and my faithful crew and I spent the best part of it living in the open grandstand at Newmarket Racecourse. Only when we'd become senior members of the squadron, ie we were well on towards completion of our tour, did we move into what was regarded as more salubrious accommodation at the Jockey Club in the town. Nevertheless, I recall with affection the spirit which prevailed on the squadron despite the wretched "domestic accommodation" — well did we deserve the appellation "The Mad Nines".

'Operations continued throughout the winter, though the weather was as great a hazard as the German defences. One night, on the way to Duisberg, we flew through heavy cloud and ice piled up on the wings; then suddenly the propellers turned blue and great sparks flew from one to the other — St Elmo's Fire, a manifestation I'd not seen before but was to encounter now and again thereafter. The ground staff too had their problems. There were no hangars at Newmarket, and the fitters, riggers, etc had to work in the open in all weathers. During that winter engine tents were placed over the Pegasus engines, with paraffin heaters inside, to stop the oil freezing. This was the only protection the fitters had, yet they survived. Places like Newmarket seemed to bring out the very best in everyone — life at the "permanent" stations didn't have the same zest.

'On 18 February 1941 something occurred which was quite outside the operational experience of the crew of "R-Robert". We were breaking in a new second pilot, doing circuits and landings at the Rowley Mile (our airfield). While taking off towards the town, with the new second dickey at the controls, I suddenly saw great gouts of smoke and debris ahead and realised that the town was being bombed. The bomb bursts were tracking towards us and I looked above them to see a German Dornier. He hadn't seen us and, after releasing his stick of HE, the pilot made a gentle turn to the left, presumably to check results. This gave me the chance to change seats with the second pilot and to close on the Dornier. We come up from underneath on his starboard side and as soon as we were close enough my front gunner, followed quickly by the rear gunner, opened fire. As we flew alongside him — for perhaps 10 to 15 seconds — he suddenly jerked and then hauled up into cloud. I pursued him but the murk was thick and I couldn't find him. After a few minutes I returned to base and reported the incident to the Flight commander, Sq Ldr J. B. Black, and there the matter might have ended. Later in the day, however, the Flight commander sent

Above: Climbing aboard. 75 (NZ) Sqn crew enter their Wimpy. Note AG carrying spare gun barrels.

for me and said a Dornier had crashed some 11 miles from Newmarket, and that the Army had reported it at low level and engaged it with light ack-ack fire. The Flight commander said no one could be positive that it was the Dornier which had bombed Newmarket, but it seemed very likely, and the thought I deserved half a "victory". Knowing how bloody awful the Army gunners were in those days, I think "R-Robert" deserved the whole victory — but who ever heard of a Wellington "fighter"? Within a day or two the incident was forgotten — we had something far more important to bother about; like surviving the rest or our ops tour. And a month later, on 17 March, my tour of duty with 99 Squadron ended, and I was told I was to go to 15 OTU, Harwell as a "screened captain" — the term then for Bomber Command skippers "resting" between operational tours.

'Before going to Harwell, however, I was to fly a reinforcement Wellington to the Middle East, so my crew and I duly reported to the Overseas Flight at Stradishall, where we took over a new Wimpy, T2614, and carried out a fuel consumption test in preparation for the trip. For some time reinforcement Wellingtons had been flown to Malta, thence to Egypt, but at Malta many had been destroyed on the ground by Ju88s operating from Sicily. The planners in Air Ministry got out their pieces of string and maps and discovered that a Wellington, carrying two overload tanks in the bomb bay, could fly

Right: Wimpy crew boarding at night, recalling Shakespeare's words. *Gentlemen of the shade, minions of the moon* (Henry IV Pt 1). *British Official*

Below right: Wg Cdr C. E. Kay, DFC (rt), OC 75 (NZ) Sqn and his second pilot at their stations. *IWM*

Left: Harwell OTU, May 1942, From left: Flt Lt P. A. Willatt, Plt Off J. R. Goodman, Flt Lt (later, Wg Cdr) P. E. Berry DFC. *Grp Capt J. R. Goodman*

Right: Brown knees. Pilot Officer J. R. Goodman with 37 Sqn, Middle East.
Grp Capt J. R. Goodman

Bottom right: Desert Warrior. Wellington 'E-Easy' of 37 Sqn. *Grp Capt J. R. Goodman*

nonstop from Stradishall to Dunkirk, thence to Marseilles, on to Algeria and ultimately to Benina airfield, near Benghazi — a trip of 11-12 hours. The 12 crews selected to make the initial trip were guinea pigs, though all had operational experience and we took-off just before dark on the night of 31 March. Eleven and a half hours later T2614 landed at Benina. In fact 11 out of the 12 landed safely at Benina; the 12th man having found himself over the sea at dawn decided to turn south and eventually motored in to Sirte airfield — where he and his crew were promptly made prisoners of war by occupying enemy troops!

'After a hurried breakfast, we flew on to Heliopolis, outside Cairo, and next day delivered T2614 to Abu Sueir, the MU near Ismailia. I was then instructed to report to HQ Middle East, where I was told that although I'd finished my tour of operations, the situation locally was serious, and for the time being I must rejoin a squadron. I elected to go to my old outfit, 37 Squadron, then based at Shallufa, at the southern end of the Suez Canal zone. I remained with 37, on desperate operations, until finally being told that my crew and I were "on rest" and would be going home to the UK.

'Thus, I only reached 15 OTU, Harwell at the end of November 1941 — some eight months after my initial posting notice. While on "rest" at Harwell, from November 1941 to August 1943, I flew three more Wimpy ops. Two of these were the "thousand-bomber" raids on Cologne and Essen in May-June 1942, while the third was a desperate business to Essen when we were almost literally shot down to ground level from 10,000ft by heavy flak. We were in Wimpy HD942 (which some idiot crashed a few days later and burnt up). However, I have one of the exhaust stubs in my possession still and treasure it; HD942 carried us gallantly to Essen and back that night and I have never forgotten her.'

Air Gunner

Steve Challen's first taste of 'action' was as an air gunner in Short Sunderlands with 201 Squadron, from August 1940. After three months of monotonous patrols and virtual inactivity, however, he volunteered for more lively employment:

'Sunderlands were a marvellous experience, but not my idea of action. My request for transfer from 201 was duly granted on 10 November 1940 I was posted to 40 Squadron, based at Wyton, Huntingdonshire. A few days after arriving at Wyton I was sent over to B Flight, which was detached at Alconbury. Here we were billetted in Alconbury House, not far from the airfield. The squadron's conversion from Blenheims to Wellingtons was proceeding quite rapidly, and in fact most of B Flight were near operational standard. The crew to which I was allocated were well through their tour on Blenheims, and were now in a hurry to become operational on Wimpys so that they could finish their tour and go on "rest duties". The captain was Fg Off Whithead. We did cross-countries, some low flying, air firing, and a height test. Then for some unknown reason I was posted to A Flight, which suited me because we were now billetted in the prewar barrack blocks of the Wyton station.

We did some ground and flying training from Wyton, which at that time was still a grass field.

'More local flying practice, a height test when we reached 15,000ft after a struggle, more practice, a load test, night flying, — we were deemed ready for operations. Each flying day then, over to Alconbury by bus unless one had one's own transport. I'd begged, then bought, an old New Imperial 250cc motor-bike from a pilot. Petrol was hard to come by, but it made me independent and able to go by the back roads to Alconbury most days. It was also useful in the evenings to get out to Huntingdon or St Ives, usually to the flicks (cinema), until one day at lunchtime when, doing a fast take-off from the front of the Mess, I met a car coming in! That ended motor-cycling until the forks were straightened.

'Sorting out of crews in A Flight went on until I was put with Plt Off "Tubby" Wills, a short, fat little man supposedly related to the Wills tobacco people. He was captain and first pilot. Fg Off "Mick" Spence, an Irishman, was the nav-bomb aimer, a peacetime RAF Observer with the appropriate "Flying Arse-Hole" O badge. The W/Op-AG was Don Pritchard. These were the Blenheim crew who were well on in their tour. The "new" boys

Below: Line-up of 40 Sqn Wellingtons at Alconbury, January 1941.
G. W. S. Challen

were Sgt Sargent, the second pilot, and the front gunner, Joe, was a peacetime wireless operator who had remustered to air crew. Joe had already completed a tour, but wished to continue at Wyton/Alconbury, because he was living with his WAAF girl-friend in the WAAF quarters (ex-married quarters) at Wyton.

'The crew, now ready for ops, continued with a few more training flights, one an oxygen test — the first time I'd experienced its use. Sgt Sargent did some circuits and bumps one day — and bumps there were. A wing dipped just enough to clip the Chance Light, carrying the top pot with us, careering down the runway with the remains perched on the wing. Wellington R1239 had to have a new outer section fitted — I didn't reckon much to our second dickey! Some leave followed in December, then more training until Christmas. Two days later — action.

'Our first novice operation was scheduled for 27 December. A night flying test (NFT) before lunch, briefing in the afternoon, all the crew. The target was Le Havre, the learner's initiation to ops. Take-off 1630hrs. Just before we made our way out to Wimpy T2515, we were issued with a flask and a bar of green foil-wrapped chocolate — the best thing ever issued. Flying clothing was just the stuff I'd been issued long ago at Manston — Sidcot, black, sheepskin-lined boots, silk gloves, leather gauntlets, helmet. We did have the parachute harness suit, known as the goon suit, which kept things a bit tidier. What a job to get into the turret, especially with the parachute pack clipped to the upper left-hand side. It was easier to get in, then lean back, bringing the 'chute forward over the top. All was not too bad once you were settled. Too much heavy breathing steamed up the perspex, which was very difficult to remove. No difficulty in locating the target, plenty of broken cloud to give a glimpse of the coast. The flak coming up was the biggest give-away. We didn't seem to spend much time identifying the aiming point before Mick Spence said "Bombs gone", whereupon Tubby made a steep turn away to sea, nose down for speed, towards home. An uneventful trip back to base and landing just after 9pm.

'De-briefing didn't mean much to me. I couldn't think of anything of importance to report. Should I describe the flak colours, the shape of the so-

called "flaming onions", the noise of near-bursts? No one ever explained why that noise sounded like marble dropping on to a drum. Most of the noise, I suspect, was the pressure vibration rattling the fabric on the stringers. There were a few small patches noticeable next time out to dispersal in daylight. Another thing I noticed was a helluva draught coming up the link chute which made my eyes water when looking through the reflector sight; I determined to remedy this as soon as I could.

'Apart from a few NFTs, then stand-downs, for the next two weeks nothing happened. We were issued with

Top: Wellington Z8736, 'Q' at Luqa, Malta, and its crew. From left: Sgts G. S. W. Challen (R/AG), Harry F. J. Gibbons (W/Op), Charles W. Ingram (Wop/AG), Paul H. Morey (Nav), R. Gordon Murray (2/P), Flt Lt K. F. Vare, RNZAF (Captain). *G. S. W. Challen*

Above: Wellington crews of A and B Flights, 108 Sqn, gather for a Press photo. *G. S. W. Challen*

29

Right: Wellington at 105 Maintenance Unit (MU), April 1942, on arrival via Malta. *E. A. Sanders*

Above: Air Gunners sorting out ammo belts for the rear turret of Z8900 of 214 Sqn, Stradishall, 1942. This aircraft had previously served as 'C-Charlie' in No 9 Sqn in 1941.

sheepskin flying suits which had plugs for heated gloves and boots. I could only just get my goon suit over the top; the zips were very difficult to start. Wilhelmshaven on 16 January 1941 in R1239 was a tryout of these gloves and boots, which seemed to get too hot. The only way to control the heat was by unplugging for a time each extremity; not an easy thing to do, especially reaching your ankle where the boot connection was located. Another ''extremity'' was equally hard to reach when you wanted to pee in the empty bottle alway carried by most rear gunners. Apart from the sheepskin trousers and parachute harness straps in the way, the centre-piece of the goon suit, about three or four inches wide, came through your legs from the back, up the front under your chin where the zips connected, and you zipped downwards to make a tight fit around the legs. Removing gloves to use the ''relief'' bottle, your hands soon became cold enough not to know when you put them back in the heated gloves whether they were hot, warm or cold. I suffered blisters on occasion through

not feeling how hot the gloves had become.

'The following day I explained to the rigger of our kite my idea for the turret bottom. The link chute came out and in its place we fitted a little hinged trapdoor made of aluminium with a felt seal. The catch was arranged so that I could operate it with my foot. All empty cartridge cases and links could then fall to the curved bottom of the turret, whereupon I could open the trap. It needed a kickabout with your feet to get rid of them all, push the trap shut and move the catch with your other foot. This trap also came in useful for usual bottle of pee and other ''presents'' I used to carry for Jerry, including half a dozen 4lb incendiary bombs. Mick Spence was always asking for drift sights, so I thought a pinpoint of light on the ground would be better than any glint of water or careless blackout to train my sight on. I used to chuck out the odd one through the hatch in the turret glazing by my right hand too; useful for taking photos with my little Zeiss Ikonta! Not much to identify on these photos except streaks of light from the searchlights, flak or fires on the ground, and very cold on the hand. What would have happened if a bit of flak had lodged in the incendiaries doesn't bear a lot of thought . . .

'A few more visits to the ''Happy Valley'' (Ruhr) followed, then on 12 March 1941 the target was announced as Berlin. The briefing room, wasn't very large, mostly taken up with tables where the navigators had their maps spread out. All crew members gathered round these tables while briefing took place. The usual guff about route in and out, searchlight and flak concentrations, expected weather, cloud, moonlight etc, and any other intelligence. Not a word about time over target — we usually just took-off and got there as soon as we could. ''Attention'' was called, the Station Commander and other ''scrambled egg'' types crowded in, and then it was realised that Lord Trenchard, "Father of the RAF", was amongst them. A little pep talk from the old boy and good wishes for our success.

'Take-off at 2000hrs. A mixed bomb load, HE and incendiaries, with the weight reduced for maximum fuel. We had an uneventful crossing until well into Germany when flak and search-lights started together. We were as high as the old Wimpy could manage with a decent load — about 12/13,000ft, and only then after a struggle. Magdeburg en route put on a real show. We'd not seen anything like the amount of light and heavy stuff coming up, some of it at our height; I could see some black "puffs" at our level, and we must have passed through some as there was an acrid smell of burnt explosive. Tubby was changing height and direction to put off any accurate prediction, and it must have worked because there weren't any bursts near us to do any damage, though that rattle on the fuselage could be heard. Then a slight lull until well over Berlin Then several groups of searchlights came on together, making it impossible to see anything downwards, or upwards for that matter, except a layer of smoke or cloud. I suppose the idea was to silhouette us against this background. Mick Spence was already on the floor in the nose at his bomb sight. "Bomb doors open" . . . a bit of "Left, left, steady" . . . and it was "Bombs gone, close doors". We were coned by lights now, causing Tubby to get a wee bit rattled until Mick got back up and gave him some reassurance and directions to get out of the cone. The Wimpy had a good testing as we did steep diving turns, climbs and other gyrations. Tubby admitted later that he really didn't know what attitudes the aircraft was in, or how we escaped a complete loss of control! It says something for the Wellington that it survived structurally without permanent warpage.

'Once out of the lights tension eased somewhat, though there was so little flak to be seen that it put us on our guard for nightfighters. I found myself staring at points of light which turned out to be stars, exhaust sparks, or simply lights reflected in the perspex. Cold was eating into me after the sweat over the target. Coffee would be welcome, so off with the gloves whilst I fiddled with the flask. Frozen slush

poured into the cup, so I put the lot into the bottom of the turret, then struggled my gloves on again and connected them. I must have left the connection in too long because I found later that the back of my left hand was blistered. No other excitements before landing back at Alconbury at 0645hrs. De-briefing took a little longer, the Intelligence Officer asking all sorts of questions before we were allowed a bus-ride back to Wyton. There was an argument about the "ops breakfast" as we coincided with the ordinary break-fast and off-duty air crew types tried to get in on the bacon and egg, rather than dried egg on fried bread.

'We operated four more times in March — Bremen and Cologne — while in the following month it was Kiel's turn, four times. Tubby, Mick and Don were nearing the end of their tour, while Sgt Sargent was made up to captain with a crew of his own, so we had a new second dickey, Plt Off Whyte. Further trips to Merignac aero-drome, Bordeaux, Kiel twice more, then the finish of Tubby, Mick and Don's tour. A celebration was in order,

Above: Mighty Wurlitzer — the rear gunner's office in a Wellington from the inside; rear defence of Wimpy N2990, which served with 115 Sqn ('P'), 11 OTU, 24 Sqn ('NQ-D' & 'ZK-9'), before being struck off RAF charge on 19 March 1943. *IWM*

so all available went off to the Golden Lion St Ives. What a send-off — all those who could piled into the bangers which passed for cars, roaring off to the pub. I remember Tubby and Hugh Lynch-Blosse doing a fiendish dance on a table top, finally collapsing on to some locals (who didn't think too much of us rowdies!). After a hectic ride back, the party continued in the sergeants' mess until the SWO (Station Warrant Officer) closed the bar and persuaded the commissioned types to stagger off to their own quarters. I never heard again of Tubby, Mick and Don, or their subsequent adventures. Joe the front gunner, finally went to an OTU instructing, when his cushy number at Wyton was rumbled. I applied for a transfer to Boulton Paul Defiants — but I'm glad I didn't get it!

'Sergeant Sargent didn't seem to gather a new, permanent crew together, consequently I, as a spare gunner, flew with some of his new faces on three ops — Brest and Hamburg (twice). His next op, with a scratch crew, ended in disaster. On return he tried several approaches but each time decided to go round again. Visibility wasn't that bad, just ground haze. Suddenly there was a labouring of engines — then portentous silence. He had crashed in a field across the road from Alconbury House, killing all on board. I then left for a gunnery refresher course. On this, all classroom work was done at Stradishall along with some static turret firing into a sandpit close by. Then three days of air

firing, flying from the Newmarket Race Course, with Spitfires and Hurricanes doing simulated attacks from all angles.

'On return to Wyton/Alconbury it seemed I was still the 'spare' gunner; no one came eagerly after my services despite my refresher course! A pilot I'd flown with just before the course and his crew, however, were without a rear gunner, who was on the sick list with eye trouble. The captain, a New Zealander in the peacetime RAF, was Flt Lt K. F. Vare, an expert pilot. Second dickey was Gord Murray, RCAF; nav/bomb aimer was Sgt Paul Morey; plus Sgts Charles Ingram from London, and Harry Gibbons from Wales. We got on well together, and after a couple of NFTs and standbys on successive days, were off to Dusseldorf. Vare proved to be absolutely unflappable, insisting that the aiming point be absolutely identified, and going around twice before he would let 'em go.

'An AMO (Air Ministry Order) had appeared on the notice board calling for volunteers for the Middle East. My new crew thought it'd be a good idea, so our names went forward. A posting came through, to Harwell. After some leave, we reported to Harwell where a new Wellington awaited us. After two consumption tests — extra fuel tanks were fitted — we took off on 26 June 1941 for Gibraltar, reaching that short, dicey runway after 11 hours in the air. A quick look up and down the main street, some snatched sleep, and morning saw us gathering tropical KD (Khaki Drill) — one shirt, one pair of KD shorts and socks. Then off from that short strip, bound for Malta. Here we were soon bundled away from the aircraft down a deep shelter operations room, where we were told we'd be leaving again that night, though not in the kite we'd brought in. So, out into the heat to move our gear into a weary-looking Wimpy. "Our" kite had already been allocated to 148 Squadron who were trying to operate a detachment at Malta. We were to fly to Kabrit in the Suez Canal zone for major maintenance, this being 148's main base.

'We took off from Luqa at 2330hrs — they didn't want us around when dawn came as there was usually an air raid then. Take-off was to the west and the old kite didn't seem to rise at all; in fact, once clear of the island it sank lower. We crossed the Egyptian coast somewhere west of Alexandria, then

Below: Rear turret in Wellington TK-T of 149 Sqn. *IWM*

south for a view of the Pyramids south of Cairo, before landing at Kabrit. Here we found there was not going to be any action for some time, so spent our days making our quarters — tents — comfortable and getting generally acclimatised. Days were spent swimming in the Great Bitter Lake, evenings in Shafto's cinema or in the mess. Some more adventurous went off on leave by hitching a lift in an aircraft which went to Tel Aviv, Palestine, once per week to collect oranges — or so they said. Suddenly, in August 1941, it was all go; pack up and move to Fayid, which the RAF was to share with the Fleet Air Arm. RAF accommodation at Fayid was unfinished, so it was tents again, and we spent some time digging in our tents, filling sandbags and building these around the tents. This latter precaution proved invaluable when one RCAF navigator used to wake in the early morning, after a night on the beer, firing his Colt 45 at rats — real or imaginary!

'On 24 September we were briefed for our first raid; the "milk run" to Benghazi. The practice was to air-test at base, then fly to an advanced landing ground, usually LG 09, top up the fuel, sometimes change the bomb load, then take-off for target later the same night. Vare was rather keen to make a good show of our first op in the Middle East, so we stooged straight over the target — supply ships against the harbour moles. There had been a few arrivals before us, so all kinds of flak was coming up and searchlights seemed to ring the town. The lights made it difficult to pinpoint anything, so round we went again. Vare decided to alter height and approach from a different direction in a shallow dive, hoping the increased speed and different height would baffle the predictors. No chance! The lights clamped on us and a coloured curtain of flak seemed to be draped around us. I'd

Above: Frazer-Nash (FN) 20A four-gun tail turret in Wellington III, X3763, KW-E, of No 425 ('Alouette') Sqn, RCAF, which failed to return from a sortie to Stuttgart on 14/15 April 1943.
Central Press

Right: Nose armament. The twin-gun turret gets a final polish of its perspex by a diligent sergeant.
Flight International

been firing short bursts on the first run, but this time I fired a longer, calculated squirt until my port gun jammed. Again, no "Bombs gone". I stripped the gun to see what the stoppage was, putting the bits with such funny names as "rear sear retainer keeper and pin" on the ledge where the sides and dome of the turret joined. Around again, lower down, and slower, from another direction. The chant began, "Left-left, right a little . . . steady". I never heard the "Bombs gone" because there was a bang, a rattle against the turret, and a smell. I put my hand out to feel where I had put my breech block bits, but only felt a breeze. Then a sensation in my throat. I wanted to cough but couldn't. I put my hand to my throat — it was sticky wet. I knew I'd been hit.

'Switching on the mike, I tried to report it but could tell there wasn't much coming from me. The crew knew something had happened, however, because Gord Murray said, "OK Steve, coming back". The turret wouldn't move by the hydraulics, so I engaged the hand gear. It needed two hands to turn the handle and move the turret central so that I could open the doors and climb out. There seemed to be a lot of lights shining on the port side — quite a hole where a lot of fabric had gone. I tried to find the stop valve for the hydraulics but it was too late; the pipes were punctured and oil was spraying all round the rear of the air-craft. I thought maybe the rudder or elevator controls were damaged, but couldn't see anything, so walked along the catwalk and met Gord on the way. I sat on the fold-down cot while Gord shone a torch on my damage. Not much to be done other than place a field dressing over the wound which I held in place by hand as I lay on the cot. The other crew members came back to have a look, though Vare seemed busy flying the Wimpy whose control wasn't quite right. With dawn coming it was light enough for me to write some questions in a diary, like

Above: 'Weary Willie' of 149 Sqn parked in moonlight at Mildenhall, May 1941. *British Official*

Left: Winter panorama. P9228, KX-Z of 311 (Czech) Sqn at dispersal, late 1942. This aircraft next went to the CGS and collided with Wellington P7530 on 13 August 1943, subsequently crashing near Lakenheath. *B. Rijnhout*

"How big is the hole in my f......
neck?'', "Where are you dropping
me?'', and "Get my kit together — keys
in the locker''. We landed at Fuka Main
at 7am, where an ambulance was
waiting. I crawled out via the belly
hatch which at one time in the design
had been intended for a "dustbin" gun
turret. Incidentally, this hatch came in
useful at a later date, when plenty of
light was needed over a target. I
arranged for extra flares, placing them
around the hatch opening clear of the
door, with cords from the fuze pins tied
to Barnes Wallis's geodetics. When the
word came, it was hatch open, one,
two, three etc, all gone in seconds, out
and burning. Couldn't say these did
much good, however; we seemed to
stooge around for a long time still
before dropping bombs.
'I was taken to 21 MRC (Medical
Reception Centre), a tented hospital in
the desert, where I was operated on by
a Sqn Ldr Wallace. Then a hospital
train to 15th Scottish, Cairo, from
where, after many examinations, I
was allowed out back to the squadron.
Got to Heliopolis and was lucky to
hitch a ride which dropped me off at

Fayid. Back at the squadron I had to
convince my skipper and the MO that
ops were the "cure" for me, because
shrapnel had severed my vocal chord
and lodged in the larynx. They
nicknamed me "Whispering Willie",
but after an intercomm test, Vare was
satisfied I was OK. We operated six
times in November — Benghazi,
Derna, Martuba, Barce railway etc —
all in Wellington Z8763. Gord Murray
was skipper on one op, but this was
scrubbed when we reached the ALG;
he did *not* like carrying our bombs
back to base and having to land with a
full load! This was our only activity in
December, because Liberators began
arriving direct from the USA, via
Takoradi, and 108 Squadron commenced gradual conversion. In
February 1942 I was back on Wimpys
for four trips; two of which were completed to Martuba airfield and the
Benina airfield near Banghazi. Both
were difficult targets to find, despite
my private brand of target-lighting.
These were my last runs as Arse-End
Charlie in Wimpys; no combats, no
bale-outs, no crashes, no casualties
(except my neck) — I was a survivor.'

Above: Wellington 1a, N2887,
of the Central Gunnery School.
Originally 'J-Jig' of 99 Sqn,
this Wimpy served at various
training units before ending up
in India/Burma, where it was
ultimately struck off RAF
charge on 26 April 1945.
C. E. Brown

Makee-Learn

Alan Butler was an Observer — the early-war equivalent of navigator-cum-bomb-aimer-cum-dogsbody in all RAF aircrews before more specifically delineated aircrew categories in bombers came into being. A prewar RAFVR member, Alan enlisted for aircrew training and, after instructional courses at Staverton, Prestwick and Bassingbourn — the latter supplying him with just eight hours night-flying experience — he was posted to No 9 Squadron at Honington in the autumn of 1940. His crew was skippered by a Canadian, Plt Off D. McIntosh (awarded a DFC in August 1941), a pilot who believed in close liaison with his aircraft's ground crew. On his promotion to Flying Officer for example, McIntosh took all his SNCO crew and the ground staff into a Bury St Edmunds pub for a celebration drink. On trooping into the pub's lounge bar with five sergeants, a corporal and several erks, he was told the bar was for 'Officers only'. He promptly walked into the public bar — followed by every officer present in the lounge bar . . .!

Butler and his crew were allotted Wellington 'P-Peter' (or 'P-for-relief' as they privately dubbed it), and duly prepared for the start of their first full operational tour. Butler takes up the story at this point:

'It was the general practice in those days to give all new ops crews what was known as a 'Makee-Learn' trip, after the skipper had done about four or five sorties as a second dickey with another, experienced crew. My skipper, McIntosh, had done two trips and, having had an outstandingly good report from Fg Off Lamb, and being dead keen himself, he asked the squadron CO, Wg Cdr E. A Healey, whether he might take us on our air "makee-learn". Accordingly, we were briefed for Schiedam, an aerodrome in Holland, which was a favourite 'soft' target for our squadron. However, weather conditions interfered and the

Below: T2468, 'Y' of 9 Sqn at Honington in August 1940. After completing 13 sorties, it crashed on 4 December 1940. *R. D. Cooling*

36

trip was cancelled. Next evening we were briefed for Schiphol in Holland, but again the weather was against us. The next day was 12 October 1940 and 9 Squadron was going to Lorient that night. McIntosh went to the CO and pleaded so hard and so eloquently to be allowed to go that Wg Cdr Healey gave his permission for us to be a standby crew, although he would not allow us *definitely* to accompany the squadron. (Healey was relatively quite old and didn't fly on ops, but always waited up until all his crews were back, and was deeply upset when any went "missing".) "Standby" meant that if any aircraft became u/s (unserviceable), instead of sending an experienced crew in the spare aircraft, the CO would let us go and thus give the experienced crew a "stand-off".

'We were duly briefed but no aircraft was unserviceable. Luck was with us, however, because Group HQ wanted an extra aircraft put on by the squadron, so the Wingco gave us the "get set". Weather conditions were the same as on the previous two days — cloud and icing — over England and a big likelihood over the whole Continent, but it was expected that there would be fairly clear skies over the target area. The actual target was the nest of submarine bays in Lorient harbour, and we had 12 250lb eggs to lay. We decided to lay them in two sticks of six if possible.

'We were airborne at 2135 and climbed to 3,000ft before signing off the R/T and setting course. Right there and then trouble began! Within three minutes, and at a height of about 4,000ft, the wireless went west — frozen up. Ice was also forming on the wings, though the de-icing equipment seemed to be working fairly effectively. We continued to climb in spite of the ice. The W/Op was working hard to get his set going; meanwhile I found out what our drift was before we got into cloud, and had just got a new course on to which we set the aircraft. Five minutes later, with a complete sheet of cloud between us and the ground and another massive and solid-looking layer above us, the W/Op told the skipper that the wireless was definitely "kaput". Navigation in those early days was very different to now; astronomical navigation had yet to make its appearance as a general practice, and dead reckoning (DR) depended on the wireless, observations by the observer-navigator on the

ground below, loop bearings, and drifts taken on the ground, usually by the rear gunner. There was no place we could use the loop on this raid, the ground was obscured, and the wireless dead — a nice problem for a brand-new observer!

'McIntosh told me to come up beside him for a moment. I knew what was coming and quickly reviewed the situation, not forgetting possible icing-up. The only thing I could do was to keep a very accurate air log and a DR position, but it *was* our first trip — turning back would only look as if we'd funked it. It came, "Can you still get us there?" I said, "I think so but there's nowhere to use the loop on. Personally I want to go, but there's a definite possibility we'll get lost". The skipper hadn't asked me this on the intercomm as he didn't want the rest of the crew to know we were in this mess yet. He

Above: Two views of Alan Butler's Wellington after the fire was doused. *Bundesarchiv*

thought for a while, then plugged in his intercomm and called up the crew, telling them that the wireless set was u/s, but that we were going on. Each man was to report everything he saw both to him and to me as it might help my navigation.

'I glanced along the wings at the ice and, touching Mac on the shoulder, pointed exultantly at them — they were now free of ice! Height 8,000ft and just entering a second belt of cloud. Would the moisture in them ice up or not? As we entered this second belt of cloud we both kept our eyes fixed on the wings... minutes passed... still we climbed, in spite of ice forming and weighting us heavily. At last good old "P-Peter" limped gamely out of cloud at 15,000ft and the de-icing gear soon began to free us. Time went by slowly... all I could do was my air plot... still solid cloud layers below us... at last we became due over Lorient. Nothing to report, nothing to be seen except cloud, cloud and cloud. Then the rear gunner spoke, "The cloud's thinner here... I think I can see the ground". I dived into the bomb-aimer's position for a look. At first I could see no difference, then as my eyes became accustomed I saw the blackness of ground below. I went and got my maps to try for a pinpoint... a few more seconds and I realised that in fact we were over the sea. I did some quick thinking and decided we must have overshot the target. I gave the

skipper a reciprocal course and just after I'd plotted it the front gunner reported flak ahead and about three degrees port. I pulled my bombing switch down in readiness and asked the skipper to put the master switch down and open the bomb doors. A few minutes later we could see fires and explosions ahead and below — it was Lorient OK. I was about to drop my first bomb on enemy territory...

'We ran up at a speed of about 130mph at 10,000ft. They were firing at us now and the skipper was jinking away from the numerous searchlights. I was having great difficulty in keeping the target area in my sight, but picked out the submarine bays and directed the skipper to steady her for a second. He did so and I corrected the course over target with a quick "Left-left". He nosed the aircraft over and began to jink again. I kept my eyes glued to the target after making necessary adjustments to the bomb sight. Just before I was about to bomb I called the skipper to keep her steady, then reached for the bomb release tit.

'"Steady... steady... steady... bombs gone!" At the very second I pressed the tit, the kite seemed to jerk unsteadily; either we had been nearly hit or Mac had started to jink again. With a sinking heart I looked down for bomb bursts. I'd missed the target! There was a spit of land jutting out into the sea just to port of our objective, and the lurch of the aircraft had flung our

Below: Sgt Alan Millington, the second pilot. In background is the famous 'Marble Arch' — Mussolini's boasted 'gateway to Tripoli'. *Bundesarchiv*

bombs to port. But I'd got *something*. I watched the bomb bursts run across that strip of land and then a series of greenish flashes shot erratically over the whole area — they looked like electrical flashes. I resolved to complete the job I'd started. I had six more bombs to drop, and this time nothing disturbed my aim. The bombs fell squarely on that strip of land with the same result as before, and now fires were springing up most successfully.

'The crew were jubilant and, as we circled so that I could observe and note the fires and damage caused by my predecessors, they were all yelling congratulations at me over the intercomm. "Can it", I said, "I missed the target". "Well chum, you sure hit something good" was the reply from Mac, and I knew then he'd back me up for dropping the second stick where I'd laid the first. I gave him a course for home.

'Reaction set in soon after I got back to my nav table. I alone knew that it was purely good luck that we had got to the target — now we had to get back . . . somehow. I was far from happy — after all, I had only eight hours' night flying experience. However, we stuck grimly to our course, keeping a sharp lookout for the French coast . . . nothing . . . just those bloody clouds again . . . time for the English coast now . . . *is* that a coastline? . . . no, just a darker cloud . . . wishful thinking. I scanned my list of beacons, those friendly lights which would tell me where I was, and picked out the most useful. I asked Mac to try to get under the clouds as we *should* be over England by now. We came out at 4,000ft this time . . . but no beacons.

'We had to turn on ETA and, sticking to my guns, I firmly gave a course on the intercomm in a confident voice — though inwardly I wondered where we were. Mac turned on to it without comment; he wasn't one to alarm the others, though he must have realised the mess I was in. Good old Mac, a blasted good skipper! "Twenty minutes late", I said, "We should see our own beacon or one nearby within five minutes. All keep your eyes open". A miracle occurred — the front gunner reported a beacon ahead. As we got nearer he gave me the letters it was flashing — it was Mildenhall, only 15 miles from our own 'drome. I told Mac to fly to it and when we got there I was ready with a new course. Meanwhile we switched over to R/T and contacted our own 'drome. After five hours and 50 minutes flying, we touched down — home again.

'We were interrogated and I explained that the first stick of bombs seemed to have caused so much trouble below that I'd deliberately dropped the second stick there. Squadron Leader Harrington nodded, and having consulted plans of the harbour said we must have hit a torpedo dump. I observed that the discharges were

Below: Sgt Steve Bevan, the rear gunner, under initial interrogation. *Bundesarchiv*

greenish and looked electrical, but he shrugged his shoulders and, pointing to the plans, said that there was nothing marked there but storehouses and shed. Late next day, however, he summoned our skipper and told him we'd destroyed the submarine wireless control station, and congratulated him. Mac was officially reprimanded for going on the trip without wireless — then privately congratulated for not turning back. I was reprimanded for the paucity of navigation notes in my log, which consisted mainly of meteorological information. I didn't care . . . we'd got there!'

From his first 'Blooding' until March 1941, Alan Butler continued on ops over Germany and France, and then volunteered for service in the Middle East zone. For this he was crewed with Sgt Alan Mackay (skipper), G. L. Millington (2nd pilot), Jim House (W/Op), Bill Ainsbury (front AG), and Steve Bevan (rear AG):

'On 19 March 1941 my crew were briefed for Malta, the first stage of our trip to the Middle East. We were airborne from Stradishall at 2150 and when no more than 100ft off the deck the air speed indicator (ASI) conked out. Our wireless was fitted up for the Middle East, as was our R/T, so we had no means of communication with the ground. Meanwhile, the aerodrome had already doused all flarepath lights. We fired off all our Very cartridges but received no answering signals from the ground. Then to make matters worse, we lost sight of the aerodrome.

'Now this was my first trip with Alan Mackay as skipper and I was curious to see how he would react. Landing an aircraft without an ASI is no joke even in daylight, when you can at least judge your speed, but landing at night in pitch blackness is a highly ticklish problem. Moreover, Mackay might be forced to put her down in any old field he could find. Would he cope as well as my old captain, McIntosh? As far as I could see, the rest of the crew — who had all done 12 ops already with him — had complete trust in him.

'Glancing at the met-forecast wind, I made a quick calculation on the CSC and told him roughly where the 'drome *should* be. We flew off and in a few minutes we managed to find the aerodrome again by means of the local church. Mackay was perfectly cool — at least, to all outward appearances —

and he told us he was about to land as best he could, and to brace ourselves for a crash. Should this occur we were to get out just as fast as possible because we were carrying 1,030 gallons of petrol and the kite was likely to catch fire. I rapidly finished off my log, then prepared for a bit of quick action.

'We were just coming up to the 'drome, and had just passed the perimeter hedge, when the lights came on for the flarepath. Mackay neatly lifted the Wimpy over a cement-mixer which might otherwise have got mixed up with our undercarriage, then made a perfect landing. I now *knew* there wasn't much wrong with my new skipper — he'd done better than finely and, though white with the strain, was quite calm. After all the explanations had been made, we trooped off to the mess to stand our skipper a few well-earned drinks, not to mention restore our own composure. Here we ran into more trouble— this time with the Station Warrant Officer (SWO), because we were in flying boots. I don't think that SWO knew just how near he was to getting thumped that night!

'Next afternoon we were briefed for Benina, near Benghazi, on the North African coast. This meant a trip of 1,920 miles, a distance only just within our flying range, leaving us no safety margin whatsoever. (It was, I believe, the first time such a trip had been attempted.) We became airborne at 1935 and set course for the English coast just near Clacton at 1940hrs. It was a very dark night and difficult to pick up landmarks. However, we were able to see where we crossed the coastline and then set course for La Carmagive, a small place near Marseilles.

'There was little to record about the actual flight. To our surprise, we were fired upon while flying over "Free France" but as we observed a large fire some 30-40 miles away to port, it's possible they had good reason for their dislike. The night was clear of cloud and, beyond temperatures etc, there was little to record in my met notes. I found we were approaching high mountains about 30 miles before we were due over our objective point and, taking a wireless bearing from Malta to check this, altered course direct for Tunisia. We duly crossed the French coast on an ETA correct to the minute and commenced the long sea-crossing. I checked all navigation for possible errors, found nothing wrong, and got ready for the next stage. Again, our ETA was correct and we made landfall on the Tunisian coast to the minute, turned on ETA inland, all according to briefing instructions.

'After setting our easterly course we crossed the coast once more and, shortly after, passed close to the isle of Lampedusa; correct for track and time. It was now too cloudy for sea drifts — cloud appeared soon after we passed Lampedusa, and within an hour put a 10/10ths blanket of cloud between us and the sea. We saw the dawn, and a wonderful sight it was. The nose of our Wimpy was more or less pointed into it, so that in spite of our tiredness we had to look at it in any case. We were at 10,000ft with complete cloud below and a little cloud above us. When our ETA arrived I had a good look below for possible cloudbreaks, and told the W/Op to get his QDM. We'd been trying to contact Benina for the last hour, but apparently there was some sort of trouble with the wireless — something broken or lost — and he (the W/Op) had been unable to make contact; unfortunate, because we only needed a solitary bearing. Therefore, there was only one thing to do — go down through cloud and find out whether we were over land or sea. So, some five minutes after our scheduled time, we broke cloud at 1,000ft — only to find we were still over sea.

'I was not, as yet, unduly worried. It was a long trip from Tunisia to Benina, and it would be quite possible to be 20 minutes or so incorrect with a bad Met wind and no navigational data — which was the position we were in. Meanwhile, for the past three hours Mackay had been having considerable troubles. The starboard wing was "heavy", and to keep the aircraft anywhere near level he was having to put his full weight on the stick. For the whole trip our second pilot had been of no practical use; he was feeling far from well and spent most of the trip on the bed. He had not actually been airsick — had he been so he might have recovered and been able to help the skipper — but he seemed unable to remain at the controls for more than a few minutes. So I contacted the rear gunner and told him we must get a drift if at all possible, in spite of the very choppy sea. I put every kind of sea marker over but, in spite of Steve's very keen eyesight, he was unable to get a very imperative drift.

'I turned back to the wireless again and asked Jim House to get a bearing from Malta, and while he tried this I discussed the situation with the skipper. There were now two possibilities. One, which I favoured, placed us down in the Bay of Syrte, while the second meant that we had passed the huge hump on the north coast of Africa and were blissfully flying on down the Mediterranean. (I think Mac thought this was the case at the time). The W/Op gave us a QDM at the same time, telling us he thought it was "fishy". After I'd asked him what he meant, he said he thought it might be a "twisted" or false bearing put out by the Germans. I didn't know what to think! Twisted bearings, second pilot ill, unable to obtain drifts, petrol running out, and dog-tired after 12 hours' flying; I was in a quandary. Anxiously I pressed the petrol gauge knobs... they *said* 60 gallons, about 50 minutes' flying... IF the petrol came through from the "heavy" wing... which I didn't think it would.

'Then Sgt Millington pointed to starboard and said, "I believe that's a coastline". Steve Bevan said he too had been watching it and thought it was coast, so I had a look through binoculars and thought so myself. We decided to edge in closer and see. It was undoubtedly land; a blessed sight since we were certain it must be in British hands as the latest news placed British positions at El Agheila, which we should have already passed. Confidently we turned in to the coast at 900ft and at about 100mph. I collected my maps ready to try to get a pinpoint, and a few minutes later we turned to port and flew parallel with the coast, about a mile out to sea, and I fixed our position at 0805hrs. Then we got it!...

'I heard a ripping sound... fabric tearing off... the starboard engine stopped... there were clouds of black smoke all around us. "Can you turn out to sea?" I asked "I'll try" answered the skipper. He presented our tail to the enemy guns and Steve, in the rear turret, took this golden opportunity to pour bullets into the range of low hills in which the enemy guns must have been situated. It was no good. We were losing height so fast there was nothing for Mac to do but make for the coast. This he did, telling us all to prepare ourselves. I went forward and let Bill Ainsbury out of his front turret, then hurried back to destroy my maps etc.

The rest of the crew were doing various things in preparation for abandoning an aircraft in enemy territory; the W/Op destroying his log, his set and any other vital instruments.

'Mac did a wonderful job. With perfect coolness, he put the undercart down and scraped on to the hardest-looking patch of sand in sight as neatly as if he'd been landing on a proper aerodrome. Personally, I feel I owe him an everlasting debt; twice in 36hrs he'd displayed coolness, courage and a quiet determination.

'We set about destroying the aircraft. The German were still firing at us; as I got out of the astro-dome a shell burst directly over my head — I jumped down rather quickly! That kite was the very devil to set on fire. We wasted a whole box of matches trying to set fire to some spare maps and papers, then eventually tried the more general method of using a Very cartridge. It was only by this last means that the Wimpy took fire. We hurriedly removed ourselves from the immediate vicinity to watch the blaze.

'We hadn't been any too soon. We could see Germans approaching from the east, while within moments it became apparent we were also being approached from the south and the west. When they got closer we realised they'd inadvertently paid us a high compliment — a great semi-circle of infantry, light tanks, armed motorcycle units, armoured cars, and several types of light machine gun carriers; I would not have been particularly surprised to have seen a U-boat pop up! They certainly seemed to have expected six British airmen — all unarmed — to cause a lot of trouble! Somewhat puffed up with pride, we stood up.'

Alan Butler and his fellow crew members were taken by truck to HQ, Afrika Korps and interrogated separately, then flown next morning by Junkers Ju52 to Tripoli. Another Ju52 took them on to Reggio, Italy, and next day onward, via Bari, crossing the Alps, and eventually landing at Munich. From here to Frankfurt, then by car to Oberursel and the Dulag-Luft. For the next four years, Butler remained a 'Kriegie' in — successively — Stalag-Luft II, Sagan, Heydkrug, Thorn, and Fallingbostel, before ultimately being liberated on the morning of 16 April 1945 by the British 7th Army Division.

Below: A more formal POW view. Standing from left: Sutherland, Alan Mackay, Steve Bevan, Bill Ainsbury, Greager. Seated; Jim House, Alan Butler, Alan Millington. *A. Butler*

By Day, by Night

John — 'Jo' — Lancaster joined the RAF with no particular desire to fly bombers, though he was eventually to fly intensive operations in the classic aircraft bearing his name. Nevertheless, his individual wishes were ignored with the delicacy of decision long associated with the RAF Record Office hierarchy of those years, and his lengthy wartime flying career proved to be wholly associated with 'heavies': 'I didn't want to be a bomber boy. In 1940, with the Battle of Britain and all that, I distinctly fancied myself as a glamorous fighter boy, and even made it as far as a fighter FTS, on Miles Masters at 5 FTS, Sealand and Tern Hill. However, I was a member of the only Flight on our course who completed the night-flying part of the syllabus, and we were all posted to bomber OTUs; in my own case to 20 OTU, Lossiemouth on Wellington 1cs. Having resigned myself to becoming a bomber type, it seemed reasonable to me that, having recently served an engineering apprenticeship with Armstrong Whitworths, helping to build Whitleys, I should transfer to the Whitley OTU at Kinloss, some 12 miles further along the Scottish coast. I gained an audience with my CO, Group Captain Smyth-Piggott, and told him so, but he wasn't very convinced. So, Wimpys it had to be — and I never regretted it from that day on.

'I joined 40 Squadron at Alconbury, and looking back on my time with that squadron it comes through as a very happy, easy-going period, which was due, I believe, mostly to the fact that our cosmopolitan crew teamed up together at OTU and quickly developed a very close bond of friendship. We all had total loyalty and confidence in each other. We were, of course, periodically scared stiff together, but at the very earliest opportunity thereafter we celebrated our 'reprieve' together in pretty good style! My tour on 40 Squadron covered the period May to October 1941. For the most part the nights were short, and quite often it was getting quite light as we crossed the enemy coast on the way home. One morning the sun was almost up as we hurried across Belgium, and we passed a Dornier going the opposite way, only about 500 yards away — presumably on his way home too.

'In retrospect it all now seems to have been very casual. By mid-morning each day we would know if ops were on or off. It was commonly said that if one visited the bar of the George Hotel in Huntingdon at lunchtime, the senior Intelligence Officer, Sqn Ldr C........., was certain to be there, and could be relied upon to disclose the "target for tonight". I never personally tested this out, but I believe it to be true. We'd carry out an NFT which usually included most of the ground as well as air crew, and invariably consisted of a beat-up at nought feet up one side of the Bedford Canals and back down the other side. These are a pair of dead straight parallel canals which run between Chatteris and Kings Lynn. We gleefully terrorised the Land Army girls and others working in the fields, and sometimes landed at neighbouring airfields to pay social calls on friends and perhaps join them for lunch. There was no specified or mandatory route to or from any target, and no specified take-off time or time over target.

'Each crew was allotted its own aircraft and the luxury of its own individual ground crew; one Fitter IIE to each engine, and two Fitter IIAs for the airframe. Here again, a

tremendous team spirit, pride, loyalty and mutual confidence was engendered. On one occasion on run-up prior to an op, there was a massive mag drop on the port engine. The fitter who 'owned' that engine, Cyril Bell, fell upon it in an absolute frenzy. This was high summer and the nights were short, so when the time came it was too late to start, we scrubbed. By that time Cyril was literally in tears. He ignored "Chiefy's" order to pack it in, and continued his frantic efforts to rectify the defect — which was in no way due to faulty maintenance — through the night.

'A few characteristics of the Wimpy 1c should be mentioned here. The

Left: Sprog. Jo Lancaster as a newly-commissioned Pilot Officer. *J. O. Lancaster*

Above: T2701, 'S-Sugar' of 40 Sqn at Alconbury 1941. On 24 July 1942, while serving with 25 OTU, this aircraft collided with DV476 and crashed. *J. O. Lancaster*

Right: Finals. Pilot's view of the final approach to Alconbury, 1941. *J. O. Lancaster*

cabin heater was a liquid heat transfer system from an exhaust pipe muff to a radiator which heated air before it was fed into the cabin. Even when it was working properly it was very ineffective, but it was so unreliable, due to a tendency to boil dry, that it was generally given up as a hopeless job. Instead, we wore most marvellous wool/silk mixture ''Long John'' underpants and long-sleeved vests, silk gloves, and full inner and outer Sidcot-type flying suits. The gunners wore electrically-heated Irvin suits. Even so, we were often extremely cold for many long hours.

'The Pegasus 18 engine was, thankfully, very reliable. This was just as well because at 925hp each, and having non-feathering props, it was really under-powered and could only manage a protracted descent on one engine — even if the Pilots' Notes said otherwise! A fairly regular event was for a valve rocker box on one of the cylinders to come adrift, which effectively put that cylinder out and resulted in quite unpleasant vibration.

Top: Embryo Wimpy crews at Lossiemouth OTU, prior to the award of wings etc. *W. Toop*

Above: OTUs did ops too. Wellington DV439, PP-D of 25 OTU which crashed in Holland on 1 August 1942, nr Loon op Zand. *G. Zylstva Collection*

Right: Crews and Wimpys of 149 Squadron prior to a raid over Germany on 10 May 1941, at Mildenhall. Nearest aircraft's insigne is a kangaroo, probably denoting an Australian skipper. *British Official*

Below right: Crew of 'H-Harry' of 419 Sqn, RCAF at Mildenhall on 9 February 1942. From left: Sqn Ldr F. W. S. Turner, Plt Off K. E. Hobson, Flt Sgts G. P. Fowler, C. A. Robson, N. G. Arthur, and H. T. Dell — all Canadians. *Public Archives of Canada*

46

The flap lever was undoubtedly responsible for a number of crashes from the overshoot condition. This lever was next to, and resembled, the undercarriage lever. It was very light in operation, and unless extreme care and finesse were exercised to make very small and momentary ''up'' selections, the flaps were liable to retract almost instantaneously, with probable catastrophic results. Eventually, a restrictor device was introduced on the flap lever to at least partially remedy this. The pilot's seat I recall as being very comfortable. One particularly good feature, never to be repeated, was a large adjustable support pad which supported each knee. Although our aircraft were fitted with an early form of auto-pilot, like the cabin heater this never worked for long, and we had to ''pole'' the aircraft manually for long weary hours, so a comfortable seat position was most welcome.

'On 24 July 1941 the *Scharnhorst*, *Gneisenau* and *Prinz Eugen* were lying in Brest and La Pallice. A small force of Halifaxes and Stirlings was despatched in daylight to La Pallice, whilst a small force of Wellingtons was simultaneously to attack the ships in Brest. 40 Squadron contributed six aircraft, including our Wimpy, T2701, ''S'', flying in two ''independent'' vics of three. The day was hot and cloudless, with thick smoke haze over southern England. The route to the target in this case was laid down, via the Scilly Isles. We went in at 10,000ft, and the sky over Brest was thick with black flak smoke. We stuck very close together, held our heads down, gritted our teeth, and pressed on in. One stray Wimpy passed from right to left underneath us with an Me 109 on its tail. Our rear gunner, Keith ''Kiwi'' Coleman, turned his turret to the port beam, and as the 109 broke off his attack on the other Wimpy in a vertical climb, Keith plastered him and the pilot was seen to bale out. On the way home we saw what was probably the same Wimpy, with its starboard engine on fire, ditch some miles off the Brittany coast. As his dinghy was stowed in the starboard engine nacelle, it was obvious that this would have been burned. I thought of dropping them our dinghy, but decided this wasn't practicable because it would almost certainly have finished up wrapped around our tailplane. Instead, we sent a radio report, though we never heard whether our valiant air-sea rescue

chaps were able to snatch them back. Short of fuel, we made for St Eval in Cornwall, as did a number of other aircraft, mostly well shot up and carrying dead and wounded. It was a fair shambles, and we all had to muck in together to help as best we could. Our little trio came through without casualty, though the aircraft were in a bit of a mess. Mine, in addition to being well perforated, had a hole through the windscreen and the hydraulic system out of action. The other Vic from our squadron broke formation and one was lost, while another suffered fatal casualties among the crew from an Me 109 attack. Having been told at briefing that there was to be a fighter escort of Spitfires, we were naturally somewhat indignant that none of us had set eyes on any Spitfire. In all fairness, however, I'm sure that we had our ''unseen'' Spits to thank for the fact that the sky had not been full of enemy fighters.

'Ice protection on the Wimpy 1c consisted of alcohol sprays for the props and engine air intakes, and alternate hot air for the carburettors. The wing leading edges were smeared with a substance popularly known as ''snowdrop grease'', which looked like marzipan, and which, of course, frequently got knocked about by refuelling hoses. I've no idea of the effectiveness of this treatment but it was never used later in the war. On the night of 30 July 1941, while on the way home from Cologne in Wimpy R1168, ''B'', I handed over control to my second pilot, Gordon Byrne, and took up station in the astro-dome. We flew into cloud and, when it became clear from the turbulence and St Elmo's Fire that we'd entered a lusty cu-nimb electrical storm, I instructed Gordon to select carb hot air and to turn 180-degrees to get out of it. When the starboard engine began to surge I decided to go forward

Below: Wimpy 'G-George' of 432 Sqn, RCAF over the unit base at Skipton-on-Swale, Yorkshire in mid-1943. *Public Archives of Canada*

Above: Wellingtons of 214 Sqn at Stradishall in 1940. Nearest aircraft is BU-V, W5442, *SRI GUROH*; a Wimpy which had previously flown three ops with 12 Sqn as PH-B. *IWM*

Above: R1448, 'L' of 218 Sqn, *AKYEM ABUAKWA*, later re-coded as HA-N. Eventually transferred to 20 OTU, it crashed on 6 August 1942. *IWM*

Right: W5361, 'C-Charlie' of 12 Sqn refuelling at Binbrook, 1942. After 18 completed sorties, it failed to return from ops on 31 May 1941. *T. Mason*

and resume control. As I passed the wireless operator, he was out of his seat, recoiling from his equipment which was all aglow. Having changed places with Gordon again, I found he had *not* selected carb hot air, and had *not* turned through 180-degrees. This totally uncharacteristic stupidity was undoubtedly the result of not having a serviceable oxygen tube, even though we were only at about 10-11,000ft. Things then started happening very quickly. The whole aircraft was aglow, it was extremely turbulent, lightning was lighting up the inside of the cloud, and after wild surging the starboard

engine died — shortly followed by the port engine. The aircraft was difficult to control and must have been badly iced up. Then there was a colossal bang and a blinding flash — obviously a lightning strike. I had to turn the lights up full and even then it seemed a long time before I could see the instruments clearly.

'As we rapidly lost height we heard the unmistakable sound of flak, too close for comfort, and could see signs of searchlights playing on the cloud base not far below. By this time — naturally — the crew had taken up their bale-out positions. We were all waiting, putting off the evil moment until the last possible second, when, having lost height down to about 3,000ft, the starboard engine suddenly showed signs of interest again. As I nursed it back to full chat, hey presto, the port engine recovered its senses too, and we were soon able to start gaining height. The jubilations which erupted were soon flattened, however, when there was no reply from Keith in the rear turret. We thought he must have baled out. Then, as I sent Gordon down to the rear to have a look, Keith came back on the intercomm. He explained that as he prepared to abandon ship, parachute pack clipped on his chest and turret turned to port beam ready to fall out backwards, he could see the altimeter which formed part of the oxygen regulator. As all was silence on the intercomm, he deduced that the rest of us had departed, but as there was still three or four thousand feet showing and the kite was quite steady — or at least, right side up — he decided to stay put until the last moment too. Then he heard one engine going again, then two, and his altimeter started to show a profit. Checking further, he discovered that in putting on his parachute pack he'd inadvertently pulled out his intercomm plug just as Gordon banged on his turret from inside the fuselage.

'About one in ten of 40 Squadron's 1cs had their normal bomb doors removed and the bomb bay faired-in, leaving a recess deep enough to accommodate a 4,000lb "Cookie". Normal max bomb load was nine 500lb, or nine SBCs (Small Bomb Containers) each housing 81×4lb incendiary bombs. The maximum standard fuel load was 750 gallons, though on some occasions we were fitted with two 140-gallon over-

load tanks in the bomb bay. We could not carry full internal fuel with a full bomb load, so a balance was decided according to the distance to target. In each wing were six fuel cells and a tank in the nacelle. The pilot's fuel control consisted of an on/off cock for each wing tank group, and a cross-feed cock. There was a panel with (I think) 12 contents' gauges — one for each cell — and all hopelessly inaccurate anyway. It was quite impossible to judge the fuel situation, so a system was evolved whereby the cock on one of the nacelle tanks could be turned on or off from the fuselage by manipulating two wires which emerged from the wing root. This tank could then be turned off during flight until, hopefully well on the way home, one engine cut, whereupon the pilot opened the cross-feed, whilst the second pilot hastily turned on the nacelle tank; we then knew we had 40 minutes in which to get down.

'Periodically we had a new second pilot, and to each one I gave a very careful briefing and demonstration of this nacelle tank operation. One of them, a rather timid, sensitive type whom I personally considered totally

Above: 149 Sqn Wellington awaiting its bomb load at Mildenhall.

Below left: R1006, 'H' of 301 (Polish) Sqn, about to be bombed up at Swinderby, November 1940. It had an ill-starred career, flying just one sortie from Bremen on 1/2 January 1941 and crashing on return. Transferred to 18 OTU, Bramcote, it then caught fire on the ground on 2 February 1942. *Central Press*

Below: Wimpy skipper. Pilot Officer J. H. Cameron from Warialda, Australia, at the controls of his 466 Sqn RAAF Wellington at Leconfield on 26 September 1943. *RAAF*

unsuited for the job was George B......... On the very first occasion when I yelled for him to turn the tank on, after a long interval, he said he couldn't find the wires! I had to hastily get the W/Op back there to do it. Naturally, I was somewhat displeased and later gave him another thorough demonstration. The next op was to Hanover on 12 August in Wimpy X3174, "X", and when this time I called for him to turn on the tank , George said "It is on — it's been on all the time". When I asked why he hadn't told me, he said, "I was afraid you'd be cross" . . . ! With finger nails bitten down to the wrists, we thankfully slid into Wyton. We found that the tank, in fact, was *not* turned on, and next day there was not enough fuel left in the main tanks to even taxy. George did more than the normal eight ops with me, and eventually — very much against my advice — was given his own crew. Taxying out for his first op as a skipper, he put his wingtip through our front turret — thereby grounding us — and did not return.

'On 25 August, in T2701, "S", we suffered our only true engine failure. With a full bomb load we had just taken off from Alconbury and were climbing away at about 750ft, when I noticed that we'd lost all oil pressure on the port engine. Oil was streaming from the engine and it shortly seized up. Fortunately, we were able to just make it to neighbouring Wyton, where we landed out of the twilight, unannounced and unscathed; a main oil pipe had fractured.

'On 7 September we went to Berlin — the "Big City" — in Wimpy Z8859, "S". Weather was clear over the target and, by the standards of those days, the attack was successful. On the way home, however, together with a number of our other aircraft, due to a big change in the forecast winds, we drifted too far north over ten-tenths cloud, and flew back over Hamburg, Bremen, Emden, Wilhelmshaven *et al.* This route suffered almost continuous flak and eventually, down on our port side, we could see the causeway which crosses the entrance to the Zuider Zee. Just as we were all distracted by this sudden glimpse, a great shower of red tracer shot just over the top of us, followed by an Me 110. We quickly went into a tight defensive left-hand turn. The Me 110 went round in a wide left-hand turn and tried another attack. We went into a steep spiral

dive, and in attempting to follow us the 110 presented a view of its belly to Keith, who raked it from end to end. It disappeared vertically into cloud at about 4,000ft. Now, the limit in speed of a Wimpy 1c was 266mph — officially. In the recovery from our dive, our airspeed was indicated as 330mph! We sustained no damage, either from the 110's efforts or by having exceeded our "limiting speed" by 25%, and arrived back at Alconbury after eight and a quarter hours in the air without overload tanks.

'The longest op we did was in Wimpy Z8859, "S" on 29 September, to Stettin. This time we had overload tanks and were airborne for nine hours and five minutes. There was little opposition over the target, and we made four ''practice bombing range'' type run-ups before Glenn, our navigator-cum-bomb aimer, was satisfied that he had got it all exactly right. Speaking of bomb-aiming, incidentally, during this late 1941 period we had to negotiate a wide belt of very efficient searchlights — the ''Kammhuber Line'' — which stretched down through Holland and Belgium. This caused us considerable disquiet. For our revenge, when the target was in the Ruhr area, we often retained one of our 500lb HE bombs and, on the return leg, made a careful run-up on one of the searchlights. They must have been able to hear it coming, because invariably the light went out before we saw the bomb burst. We normally carried a few empty bottles which the second pilot would drop down the flare chute, and when I'd been a second pilot I'd taken great satisfaction in dropping bricks, marked ''London Brick Company'', taken from a pile adjacent to our dispersal pan.

'Having completed 31 ops with 40 Squadron, I was posted for the statutory year of OTU instructing to 22 OTU, Wellesbourne Mountford. In May 1942, still a screened instructor and still on Wimpy 1cs, I was roped in for the first of ''Butch'' Harris's ''Thousand-bomber'' ops, target Cologne. I was given a screened navigator and wireless operator, plus two pupil air gunners, while the aircraft, X9932, ''X'', was one normally engaged on dual circuits and bumps

training. It still had its dual controls fitted, which made entry and exit rather difficult — particularly if one was in a hurry. We took off in very grotty weather but on the return trip the weather was fine as, with dawn breaking, we cruised back towards Wellsbourne Mountford at about 1,000ft. The W/Op, Flight Sergeant Harrison, came up forward to sit beside me and we were enjoying a cigarette when — I think almost simultaneously — we saw the starboard engine oil pressure gauge drop abruptly to zero. Fortunately, Harrison was a very experienced Wimpy man and knew exactly what to do. He dashed aft and started to transfer oil from the 14-gallon reserve oil tank by hand-pump, and the oil pressure quickly recovered. The engine had drunk its normal oil capacity of 17 gallons in less than five hours' flying. Two nights later we took the same aircraft to Essen, but this time we didn't wait for the starboard engine to consume all its oil before replenishment.

'In October 1942 I returned to the operational scene proper by joining 12 Squadron at Wickenby, where I did three more ops in Wimpy IIIs before we converted to Lancasters. These Wellingtons had Hercules XI engines with feathering props, which transformed the Wimpy into quite a ''hot ship''. After 12 Squadron, I went back on to Wellingtons for a short period with No 1 Group's 1481 Gunnery Training Flight at Binbrook, where we flew Wimpy IIIs and Xs. With these I discovered that at low airspeeds there was a slight overbalance on the rudder, so I made a habit of very steep power-off sideslip approaches using full rudder deflection — quite spectacular when seen from the ground, I was told. However, the Wimpy really had no aerodynamic vices. From Binbrook I finally achieved my ambition of a posting to the A&AEE where, incidentally, I did some flying on the big sister Warwick aircraft, but my association with the dear old Wimpy was not completely over because early in 1946 I was seconded to Boulton Paul's at Wolverhampton for a few months. There, amongst other jobs, I did some production testing of a small number of Wimpys, modified from Mark Xs and 19s as flying classrooms — virtually the forerunner of the later Varsity, I suppose.'

Webfoot Wimpys

The contribution of the Wellington to the unceasing maritime war against marauding enemy submarines received minimal publicity during — or for that matter, since — World War 2. Yet 'salty' Wimpys played a significant part in the eventual defeat of the ocean wolves, destroying or at least seriously damaging a minimum of 51 submarines during 1942-45, and doubtless — if unconsciously — preventing or dissuading unknown numbers of possible attacks on merchant shipping convoys merely by their ever-vigilant presence. As with all Coastal Command operations, irrespective of aircraft type, anti-submarine patrol work was an accumulation of endless hours of 'watching water'; monotonous flying which rarely produced even a sniff of a U-boat, let alone any form of visible success. It was a task requiring stoic patience and physical endurance, combined with a talent for instant reaction on those rare occasions when a submarine was spotted.

One vital ingredient of success was the Leigh Light; a moveable swivelling searchlight remote from the cockpit — usually, in a Wellington, in the mid-belly position — for night illumination of any detected, surfaced U-boat. No 1417 Flight RAF was formed at RAF Chivenor, Devon, to develop the Leigh Light Wellington and to form the nucleus of No 172 Squadron as the first Leigh Light unit for maritime operations. Among the first air crews posted in was Donald Fraser, whose account of those embryo days follows:
'I was an RCAF Warrant Officer 1st Class pilot with No 150 (Wimpy) Squadron in RAF Bomber Command when I was posted in early February 1942 to 1417 Flight of Coastal Command Development Unit. I was not enamoured with the Wellington aircraft, and was looking forward to a new challenge. My arrival at Chivenor, late Sunday night, 8 February 1942,

was not very auspicious. I learned immediately that in the Chivenor Beaufort OTU there had been three fatal crashes during the past two nights. Therefore, I was relieved somewhat when I was told, next morning, that 1417 Flight was *not* connected with the OTU, but was a "hush-hush" unit located in a far hangar. Imagine my reaction when I first saw the plane, a white Wellington with porcupine-like vertical and horizontal aerials sticking out of the fuselage, and two forward-pointing Yagi aerials under the wings. There was no nose turret, but the front was covered with perspex to give a greenhouse appearance — Leigh's invention was ready for practical testing.

'I soon realised that most Coastal Command pilots had trained on other types of aircraft and that the unit was anxious to have somebody with flying experience on Wellingtons. An outline of problems involved in U-boat detection and destruction was presented by the commanding officer, Wing Commander Jeff Greswell. U-boats in early 1942 were crossing the Bay of Biscay at night with impunity on the surface on their way to their second "Happy Time" where they could attack undefended shipping off the coast of the United States of America. Airborne radar (ASV) had already been installed in the Wellington and had permitted homing-in on surfaced U-boats, with a maximum detection range of about seven miles. But frequently, with a sea running, in the last mile contact was lost due to sea return on the radar screen. Hence the Leigh Light, which was installed in the mid-under turret position.

'The next four months were devoted to intensive training. The effective operation of the searchlight had to be co-ordinated with its controls mounted in the nose of the aircraft. The Light was to be lowered below the fuselage when ASV contact was made, and swung back and forth, up and down, until the object of the ASV blips was detected. The Helwick Light Vessel in the Bristol Channel served for practice detection at night. Practice bombing was done against a floating target off the steep cliffs of North Devon; the aircraft would approach from the land, dive towards the floating target to simulate an attack on a surfaced U-boat from 1,000ft altitude and one mile distance. This training was not without its casualties. One Wellington, with the squadron's gunnery and navigation officers, a Flight commander, and a full crew, homed in on a blip which they thought was the Helwick Light Vessel. Unfortunately, the blip was an American tanker steaming up the Bristol Channel. Its

alert crew opened fire — the burning Wellington fell into the sea. There were no survivors.

'Originally there was only one Wellington with Leigh Light available for training purposes. Greswell sent a signal to Group HQ "Request some operationally-tired Wimpys from Bomber Command to familiarise our pilots flying the Wimpy and to perfect their low-level bombing techniques". Gradually more Leigh Light Wellingtons became available, but slowly, ever so slowly. Their assignment priority seemed obvious; the first to the Wing Commander, the next two to the Flight commanders, the fourth to Pilot Officer Blackmore, an experienced CCDU pilot. Warrant Officer Fraser was, naturally, further down the list. Another

Top: Leigh Light Mk XIV Wellington of Coastal Command, with underwing rockets. *via S. Howe*

Above: Mk XIV Wellingtons of Coastal Command about to start a submarine patrol. *IWM*

Canadian, Plt Off Russ, arrived, and he was assigned to fly as second pilot and searchlight operator with Plt Off Blackmore's crew. Russ was first on a short ferry flight to St Eval in Cornwall. It was a misty day, his plane disappeared. The following week the wreck was found on the cliffs behind Hartland Point, near Chivenor. I had by then my own crew but no aeroplane, so I immediately volunteered to fly with Blackmore in Russ's place until I got my own aircraft.

'Training went on. Squadron Leader Leigh periodically showed up on the station to oversee developments. The three-tiered bomb bay held the four Torpex-filled depth charges, the long case of batteries for the searchlight, and an overload fuel tank. The Wellington flew tail down even with trim. Blackmore and I worked on an obvious solution, moving the batteries into the nose of the machine. A wooden case for the 14 batteries was built under the searchlight operator's seat in front of the pilot. The aeroplane now flew better. With an all-up weight of 33,000lb, the two 980hp Bristol Pegasus engines were severely tested. Even in Bomber Command the same aircraft had an all up weight of only 29,500lb. The unfavourable power/weight ratio affected the single-engine flying characteristics of the aircraft, but this was later rectified when 1,425hp Hercules engines replaced the old Pegasus plants. It had taken four months — perhaps not really very long under the circumstances — but by early June 1942 the Leigh Light Wellingtons were ready to be tested in battle.

'The first operational sorties of 172 Squadron were flown by four aircraft on the night of 3/4 June 1942, and Greswell was the first to draw blood, flying aircraft "F". As he homed in on an ASV blip near the coast of Spain, he lowered his searchlight and illuminated a submarine dead ahead. He overshot it because his altimeter had given a wrong altitude, due to changing barometric pressures this many hundreds of miles from base. (It was some months later before a radio-altimeter corrected this problem.) On his second run-in the submarine fired recognition signals into the air. Was it a British sub? Then Greswell recalled that British submarines never shot up recognition signals, but burned flares on the surface. He attacked, dropping a stick of Torpex depth charges across the submarine's bows.

'The effect of Greswell's attack is best described directly from the log of the Italian submarine, the *Luigi Torelli*, of the 1,200-ton Marconi class. On the night of 3/4 June 1942, on a true course of 264 degrees and at a speed of nine knots, latitude 44° 43' N, longitude 06° 46' W, it was surprised by the first Leigh Light Wellington at 0227hrs. The captain of the *Luigi Torelli* [Lt-Cdr Augusto Migliorini] reported a sudden appearance of a huge searchlight on a low-flying plane. It illuminated an area about 300m to the right of his bow, then centred upon him. Immediately the navigation officer on duty gave orders to steam full speed ahead and turn to the left. However, the aircraft kept overhead with its light on the submarine. Finally, it was switched off. The night was very dark with no moon,

Above: Stickleback. Mk VIII Wellington, W5674 with ASV Mk II antennae and aerial masts, believed to have served with 331 Squadron. *MOD (Air)*

Right: Mk XIVs (NB895, 'G', nearest) of 38 Squadron. *P. H. T. Green*

Bottom right: Wellington GRXIV, LB129/G at the TRE.

but much phosphorescence on the sea. Now the captain reduced his speed to a minimum, believing that the aeroplane was detecting him by his phosphorescent wake. As he prepared to dive the searchlight of the aeroplane lit up again his stern from the right side, approximately 300m away, then centred on the conning tower of the submarine. The captain turned to the right and gave orders to open fire with the anti-aircraft guns. The plane passed over him low (250ft height) also firing, then turned off its searchlight again. When the captain thought that the aircraft had lost him because of his small wake he gave orders for a rapid dive.

'But all was not over. While the captain still had his head stuck out of the hatch, the submarine was again illuminated from a very close range. The bosun had signalled with the hooter to dive, when the captain gave orders to turn to port. Only seconds later the ship was bracketed by a stick of 250lb depth charges that exploded under its hull. The *Luigi Torelli*, covered by columns of water, jerked violently and went down by the bow. As a result of the explosion the catch freed itself from the hook and the hatch closed by itself over the captain's head while the diesel motors were still running. This created a very strong decompression before the motor could be stopped. The captain therefore introduced air into the chambers with the watertight doors near the bow to equalise the air pressure. Although out of the immediate line of fire, the *Luigi Torelli's* troubles were still not over. In some three minutes the conning tower hatch cover opened again and the

bosun's mate, who was still *outside*, told the captain that the aeroplane was still near; it had passed over twice, firing its machine guns.

'The captain's Log gives the damages resulting from Greswell's attack:
* Breakage of a considerable number of battery elements that resulted in leakage of acid.
* Fire in the chambers of two batteries, accompanied by smoke in the chambers over the batteries.
* Complete loss of power.
* Damage to compass and steering apparatus.
* Some development of chlorine.
* Breakage of shelves and fixtures.
He considered the condition of the

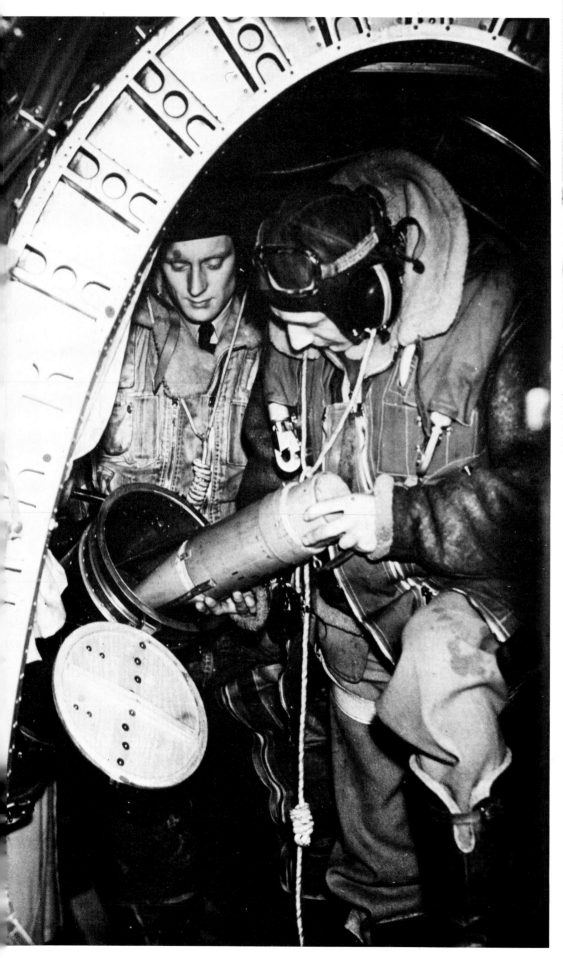

Left: Dropping a flame float for checking drift over the North Sea. *British Official*

Above: Sound & fury. NB773, RW-O of 36 Sqn taking off from a snow-bounded runway at Chivenor, February 1944, piloted by Flt Lt Look. *G. Jones* interior of the *Luigi Torelli* and decided to steer to a French port (St Jean-de-Luz). The battery fire was not extinguished or even diminished, and strong smoke was produced mainly in the wireless cabin and the officers' and NCOs' quarters. Repeated attempts to enter the front chambers with extinguishers failed. The captain ordered flooding of the ammunition store in the bow after retrieval of the cannon shells, and at length the fire was extinguished.

'In the meantime Greswell and his crew spotted a second submarine nearby. He is now of the opinion that it may have never seen him because it was submerging when spotted with ASV and searchlight. What saved both these submarines was the failure of the pursuer to get a signal of the attack to the other three Wellingtons on patrol in the area, and home them to the place of the attacks. I was second pilot and searchlight operator on the nearest Wellington, and can testify that no message of this attack was received. Undoubtedly the coded signal "472" ("Sighted sub. Am attacking") had been sent to base at Chivenor, though it may not have reached there immediately because of the low level at which the aircraft was flying when the signal was sent or because of atmospheric disruptions. This weakness in communication was later rectified, when attacking aircraft remained in the vicinity of the attack as long at their petrol supply would permit in order to home other aircraft into the area.

'In any case, the *Luigi Torelli*

escaped. Other submarines later attacked by Leigh Light-equipped anti-submarine aircraft were not that lucky. Shortly after, my own connection with 172 Squadron ended when, in mid-August, I was commissioned and posted to Wick, where another Leigh Light Wellington squadron, No 179, was then forming.'

The *Luigi Torelli* was to have a long and chequered career after this first encounter with 172 Squadron. On 5 June 1942 she was hastily repaired in a Spanish harbour, left this haven on 6 June, only to be attacked twice by Sunderlands of No 10 RAAF Squadron and further damaged. Putting in to the Spanish port of Santander, the submarine was officially interned; yet a month later made a dash to freedom. In 1943 it went to the Far East, was taken over by the Germans after Italy's surrender and retitled UIT-25; then when Germany surrendered in May 1945, was retaken-over by the Japanese who titled her RO-504. Four months later she fell into American hands, but was finally scuttled by her ultimate (sixth) captain in 1946. 172 Squadron's first true kill was to come just four weeks after Greswell's blooding attack, on 6 July 1942, when an American pilot in the unit, Pilot Officer W. Howell in Wellington "H" sunk the U-502.

The successes of the Leigh Light Wellingtons were to continue until the final victory in Europe in May 1945; with the final confirmed U-boat sinking by a Wimpy occurring on 2 April 1945 when Wellington 'Y-Yorker' of No 304

(Polish) Squadron sank the U-321 at
the location 50°N, 12° 57′ W. Indeed,
as merely one example of the sustained
effort made by the maritime Wellington squadrons, the record of No 304
Squadron shows that during its three
years' sojourn with Coastal Command
its crews had flown 2,451 sorties,
accumulating therein 21,331
operational flying hours. During these
they attacked 34 U-boats and sighted
nine others, had 31 combats with
German fighters, and lost 106 aircrew
men killed or missing. In balance the
Poles of 304 Squadron could claim just
two U-boats destroyed and a third
seriously damaged. The first confirmed
sinking came on 18 June 1944, when
Flt Lt J. Antoniewicz, skippering
Wellington 'A-Able', destroyed the
U-441, killing its captain
Kapitanleutnant Klaus Hartmann and
his entire crew.

U-441 was nearing the end of a two-
weeks patrol, and some 50 miles from
its intended haven at Brest when it had
the misfortune to cross the path of
Antoniewicz's Wellington; the aircraft
having had a complete breakdown in
its radar-search equipment, and
merely relying on the 'Eyeball Mk 1'
for the completion of its patrol in the
bright moonlight. What followed was
contained in the prosaic terms of the
Wellington skipper's official report of
20 June:

'Wellington A/304 on A-U patrol "V"
was flying on course 324deg(T) when
at 2254hrs (on 18 June) Captain
sighted 050deg, red, four miles, a tin
trail of vaporous grey smoke on the
sea. Weather was fine, visibility four-
five miles, sea calm, 9/10ths cloud at
2000ft. Captain was just about to alter
course to investigate when he sighted
045deg, green, three miles, black
object which he identified almost
immediately as the conning tower of a
surfacing U-boat. He turned to port to
get on an attacking course. At the same
time he lost height. He approached
U-boat on a course between 060 and
090(T). When one mile away 2nd pilot
and radar operator, in the astrodome,
sighted another U-boat which had
apparently just surfaced 10deg, green,
1½ miles away. Captain kept on his
course to attack first U-boat, which
then started to submerge slowly. At
2257hrs six DCs were dropped from
100ft, spaced 60ft, and set to 14-18ft,
155deg, green to U-boat heading. Rear
gunner distinctly saw positions of
entry, the first two hitting the water to

starboard quarter of UB (No 2 about 10 yards away from hull) and the remainder across the UB and on its port bow. Then he saw them explode, and the explosions and plumes completely obscured UB. He also saw a long black pipe-like object blown about 100ft into the air with the DC explosion. When the explosion plumes subsided there was no sign of the UB, and the conning tower was only just visible when the DCs were dropped. Aircraft then returned to port. Almost immediately after the attack the second UB was seen to submerge. One minute later the aircraft tracked over the scene of the attack and saw:

'(1) Two flame floats burning about 500ft apart
'(2) Between the flame floats a spreading bubbling patch of oil
'(3) Close to the second flame float two dark cylindrical-looking objects about 30ft long
'(4) A considerable quantity of smaller pieces of wreckage between the flame floats

Regarding the bubbling oil patch, this was first seen by radar operator in the astrodome as soon as DC explosion had subsided. Aircraft made three more runs over the scene, and during the second run (1½mins after the first) the oil seemed to be gushing to the surface and spreading outwards into a circle fringed with iridescence. At the third run (about 2½mins after the second) the bubbles and gushing had ceased, and the oil patch exceeded in size the area of 500ft between the flame floats. During the fourth run the oil patch was still spreading, and the wreckage described above was still evident.

Having dropped marine markers, the aircraft then set course on patrol at 2312hrs.'

If Wellingtons were prominent in the unending campaign against the U-boat in European and Atlantic waters, they were not the only active or successful Wimpys in this role. One example of Wimpy labours in the 'side-show' zones of operations was No 621 Squadron. Formed initially at Port Reitz, Kenya, in September 1943 and equipped with Wellingtons for general reconnaissance of the approaches to the Red Sea et al, 621 was based at Aden by early 1944 with various detachments in the area. Their operational area was vast, including the Persian Gulf, while enemy activity was by no means minimal; in January 1944 alone, 16 sightings of U-boats were reported.

On the morning of 2 May 1944, Wellington 'T-Tommy' of 621 Squadron was carrying out an anti-submarine patrol just south of the Gulf of Aden. Skippered by Flt R. H. Mitchell, its other crew members were Warrant Officer Harvey Riddell, the Canadian second pilot, Flt Sgt O. Gomersal (Nav), and two W/Op AGs, Sgts W. R. Stevenson and S. Philips. They could hardly believe their eyes when they suddenly came upon a U-boat, fully surfaced and steaming along at about 12 knots. Swinging immediately into an attack run, Mitchell bore in for the kill. The U-boat was U-852, commanded by Heinz Eck, which had been active in the area for several weeks, and on spotting the incoming Wimpy, Eck gave immediate orders for a crash-dive — too late. At 800 yards range the Wellington's front

Above: DWI Wellingtons on patrol in the Middle East. Nearest, L4374 originally flew with 149 Sqn in the UK, and was ultimately lost over the Mediterranean on 31 January 1942. *F. Spelman*

guns opened up, slashing a hail of bullets round the conning tower, and at 50ft a stick of six depth charges was placed with deadly accuracy up-track, two of these at least falling within lethal range of the sub's hull. The damage caused was severe enough to prevent the U-boat submerging, and she wallowed helplessly on the surface.

Signals were sent from Wimpy 'T-Tommy' for assistance in finally 'nailing' the sitting duck, and six further attacks by aircraft from Nos 621 and 8 Squadrons were made during daylight hours; each attack being fiercely contested by the crippled U-boat's gunners. Meanwhile HMS *Falmouth*, at the time of 'T-Tommy's' initial attack escorting a convoy from Mombasa to Aden, was ordered to leave the convoy and proceed to the scene. Early next morning, the U-boat was sighted and before *Falmouth* could reach her, Eck ordered the submarine to be scuttled and set on fire, while surviving crew members made for the nearby shore. Here they later surrendered to a naval landing party.

The aftermath was the award of a DFC to Flt Lt Mitchell and a DFM to Sgt Stevenson; while the U-boat commander and two of his senior officers were eventually sentenced to death by a military court in Hamburg after the war for the murder of British and Allied seamen from the steamer *Peleus* which U-852 had encountered only weeks before its ultimate action.

Peter Brewster was a Wop/AG with No 612 (County of Aberdeenshire) Squadron, AAF from March 1944 to February 1945:

'My crew was John Saul (skipper), Jack Church (2nd pilot), Jack Royans (Nav), Bill Bates, Fred Floyer and myself, all Wop/AGs, and we crewed up at No 6 (C) OTU, Silloth, near Carlisle in November 1943, where we flew many of the earlier marks of Wimpy. On posting to 612 Squadron we began flying Leigh Light Wimpys fitted with Mk 3a radar, initially operating from Chivenor over the English Channel and the Bay of Biscay, covering the D-Day operations. The radar was quite unique in those days, being a radial time-base with aerial situated in the nose of the aircraft; the front turret having been removed and replaced with a single 0.50 Browning machine gun on a free mounting.

'The Leigh Light was hydraulically operated and lowered from the dorsal turret position about halfway along the fuselage — usually by the wireless operator. The operator, being the second pilot, when operating the Light, lay in the bomb-aimer's position, on top of the Light's batteries. The Wimpy was also fitted with a radio altimeter in order that an attack on any U-boat could be carried out accurately from a mere 50ft altitude.

'After D-Day, because of our sensitive radar, we were posted in September 1944 to Limavady, Northern Ireland, to combat the *Schnorchel* being used by U-boats in the North-West Approaches. Our radar was capable of picking up an echo from what amounted to a drain-pipe sticking-out of the sea. Soon after, however, we moved again, this time on 18 December 1944 to Langham, Norfolk, where we adopted an anti-shipping role, operating from the Hook of Holland to the German coast, and attacking convoys which were apparently supplying German forces in their attempt to break through the Allied lines in the "Battle of the Bulge". Again, the radar played an important role because not only was it accurate, but also released the bombs on to target automatically. The only problem was that the aircraft had to be flown at a maximum height of 1,250ft for the accuracy to be maintained. In this job we were supported by Beaufighters and Mosquitos with rockets and cannons of New Zealand squadrons when we carried out attacks known as "Percolating". In short, after bombing a convoy we called up the New Zealanders and, after laying an artificial moonpath, they would attack with their RP and cannons.'

Also based at Langham, from November 1944 to May 1945, was Andrew Hendrie, a Wop/AG with No 524 Squadron:

'I flew Wellington XIVs with 524 Squadron as a W/AG, with Fg Off Lister as captain for most trips. Operations were against E-boats, which would attempt at night-time, and at an esimated 50 knots, to come over from the Dutch coast to the Humber estuary or off Harwich to attack our shipping. Our patrols were off Dan Helder, Ijmuiden, Rotterdam and Frisians. At briefings, therefore, areas of flak concentrations were usually stressed. We lost a lot of crews through aircraft going in too close to the coast. The first comment made to me by the squadron adjutant on joining 524 was, "Have you a car? There are so many here, and the former owners are now unknown". We had a Wellington detachment at Dallachy, home of a Beaufighter strike wing, whose role was to act as pathfinders by circling an enemy convoy, dropping a series of flares, to light the way for the Beau boys. At least, this was the proposal towards a three-squadron Beaufighter strike, escorted by Mustangs, which went to Norway. The Mustang "escort" circled the wrong enemy fighter aerodrome — thankfully, the Wimpys' part was called off!

'I recorded only one successful attack against E-boats. This was on 6 April 1945 in Wimpy NB772, skipper Flt Lt Meggison, with take-off from Langham at 0045hrs. The wake of E-boats could be seen easily in bright moonlight, giving an indication of their speed. We found three of them. We gained height to about 6,000ft, the minimum specified altitude, otherwise we'd blow ourselves up too. If memory serves me, we dropped a stick of six 250lb bombs, intended to explode in mid-air and provide a wide "shrapnel" effect. The E-boats would almost certainly have seen us, despite our black camouflage, in the bright moonlight, and they opened up with their single cannons fitted in the stern of each craft. We were hit only once when there was a brilliant flash near the rear turret. The gunner hadn't fired — he wanted to keep our position secret — and we thought we'd lost him. On return to base, we found quite a neat hole in the tail plane, which had missed the elevator mechanism by merely an inch or so.

'One experience of purely personal interest was the night of 7/8 March 1945, when we spotted V2 rockets being launched from the enemy coast area. That night one landed near my home at Hornchurch and brought half of it down — meaning there was a good chance I'd seen the launch of the actual V2 which blasted my own home!

'Regarding the Wellington, frankly, I didn't like it; especially after flying Lockheed Hudsons with two previous squadrons. I rather think my reasons were that it was night work instead of day, meaning the crew members were away from each other, giving a feeling of isolation. They were also fitted with Marconi radio, whereas most of the Hudsons I'd flown in had had Bendix radio which was much easier and more precise in tuning. In Hudsons all could and did take an actual part in flying the aircraft; this we could never do in Wellingtons. Another thing, at that time over the North Sea, we experienced on occasions quite severe icing on props and leading edges, whereas Hudsons, even over Norway, seemed to keep relatively free of such troubles.'

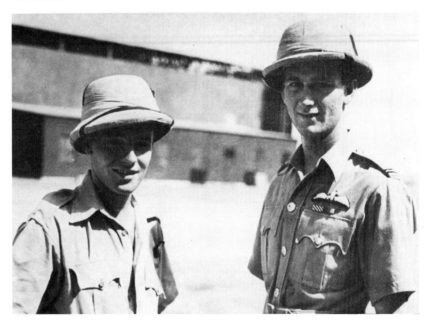

Below: Flt Sgt W. R. Stevenson (left) and Flt Lt R. H. Mitchell, DFC of 621 Sqn, Aden, 1944. *W. R. Stevenson*

Bottom: Awards of DFC and DFM respectively to Flt Lt R. H. Mitchell (shaking hands) and Flt Sgt W. R. Stevenson (4th from right), 621 Sqn, Aden, 1944. *W. R. Stevenson*

Above: GRXIVs of 304 (Polish) Sqn on 25 April 1945. *IWM*

Below: A GRXIV and its crew of 304 (Polish) Sqn, 1945. *IWM*

Fishes and Photos

Having been designed as a bomber, the Wellington is most usually remembered or regarded in such a prime role. Yet the versatile Wimpy's distinguished Service career was to include many equally important roles imposed upon it during 1939-45. Just two such operational facets were torpedo-bomber and photographic reconnaissance. Group Captain M. J. A. Shaw, DSO — 'Mike' — joined the RAF initially in April 1938, and from 1941-45 was to be associated with the Wimpy in both of these specialised operational uses for the Wellington. His introduction to the design came in August 1941, when he was posted to No 1 Torpedo Training Unit at Abbotsinch:

'My first Wellington was a Mk VIII, and my first impression was that it was much bigger and heavier than the Beaufort I had been used to up to then. I soon found, though, that the Wimpy could be thrown about pretty well and the brief trials we carried out indicated that the tactics used for Beauforts were applicable to the Wellington as far as training for torpedo operations were concerned. It was, to me, a very comfortable aircraft to fly, and the only minor vice was the change of trim when the flaps were put down. However, one soon got used to the need to ensure that the tail trimmer was adjusted before selecting flaps.

'Moving the following month to Limavady, and later Turnberry, in the six months that I commanded the Torpedo Training Squadron of No 7 (Coastal) OTU, we found the Wimpy an excellent aircraft for the job, bearing in mind that we were training crews primarily for *night* torpedo operations. I remember noticing quite a difference the first time I flew a Wellington with a full load of two torpedoes. The extra weight certainly made itself felt, both on take-off and in general handling, but they were splendid aircraft for low flying over the sea — very stable, with adequate, though not superlative, visibility from the cockpit.

'I was next posted to command 221 Squadron at Luqa, Malta, and arrived in Malta in June 1943, after the fiercest part of the war in the Mediterranean was over. We had a few torpedo trips — all at night or at dawn — but enemy targets by then were few and far between. After the Allies invaded Italy in September 1943 we came to be used more and more for

Above: Fish Porters. Lining up the two-torpedo load for a ship-hunter Wellington in the Middle East.

Left: Group Captain Mike Shaw, DSO
Grp Capt M. Shaw

anti-submarine work, at night, and my main recollection of that tour is of doing long trips on convoy escort, starting at dusk and going right through until after dawn — sometimes as long as 12 hours. A member of the crew had to pump oil through to each engine from a tank in the fuselage every hour — a tedious business. We carried a second pilot whose main function was to take the controls for an hour or so to enable the captain to have a rest on the camp bed rigged up halfway down the fuselage. Some of those second pilots had not been taught to fly Wellingtons — they might have had a bit of a problem landing the aircraft if anything happened to the captain!

'These aircraft were, of course, the Hercules-engined Mk XI, XII and XIV Wellingtons — much more powerful than the old Pegasus versions I'd flown back in the UK. Their single-engine performance was much better too, which was a considerable consolation. I found the Wimpy quite unpleasant when flying in the bumpy conditions sometimes met in electrical storms at certain times of the year in the Mediterranean, and remember having to return early from patrol on two occasions due to extremely bad weather conditions. Overall, though, my memories of the Wellington during my 221 Squadron tour are pleasureable. Although a fairly sedate old lady, it had a fair turn of speed and was very easy to fly. We were also used for occasional bombing missions at night, using flares to illuminate targets, which were confined to roads, railways and bridges near the coast of Italy. These were mostly carried out from fairly low altitudes — below 1,000ft — doubtless because we did not carry oxygen!

'My final tour of operations in

Top: Wellington XIII, JA416, 'L' of 221 Sqn over Malta on 3 January 1944. Grp Capt M. Shaw

Above: 221 Sqn Wimpy doing a 'runner attack' on a British destroyer off Malta, December 1943. Grp Capt M. Shaw

Left: Yet one more victim of Malta's 'runways' . . . R. Slater

Wellingtons, from June 1944 to August 1945, was with No 69 Squadron of the 2nd Tactical Air Force (TAF). The squadron was reformed at Northolt in May 1944 to provide night visual tactical reconnaissance in support of the ground forces during the invasions of France, Belgium, Holland and Germany. Specially modified Mk XIII Wellingtons were used and these had clear perspex noses fitted to facilitate visual observation, together with a moving film camera, and a pistol discharger for letting off photo-flashes, so that photographic confirmation of visual sightings could be provided, and finally a flare chute for launching the load of 54 flares.

'One of the bonuses stemming from the selection of the Mk XIII Wimpy was the relative quietness of the aircraft, from the ground observer's point of view. I'm certain that this characteristic enabled us to achieve a modicum of surprise, particularly when operating on moonlight nights where flares were not required. Which was just as well because we were operating at pretty low level — below 3,000ft — and often ran into heavy ground fire from the German flak gunners. The Wimpy turned out to be an excellent aircraft for the job, and I certainly enjoyed that tour very much. We normally flew with a crew of five, giving several pairs of eyes to carry out the recce task. We were part of No 34 Recce Wing — along with No 16 Squadron (Spitfires) and 140 (Mosquitos) — and while the rest of the Wing provided plenty of recce by day, the gap, as far as the army was concerned, was what happened at night. There was little tactical recce by night — and by tactical I mean right on the front line and just behind it — so the Wimpy filled this gap. We were usually given a length of roadway or canal or railway within 20 miles of the front line, and had to go and survey this more or less all night to see if there was any enemy movement, transport, troops, etc.

'We did this normally from very low level, dropping flares at about 3,000ft and then circling down below these to see what was revealed. If anything interesting was seen we were supposed to take photographs with the special camera; an open shutter type with a moving film linked to the pistol discharger, which was a sort of ''Mickey Mouse'' box with (I think) 12 photo-flash cartridges (same size as the Very

Cartridge). These latter were small and did not give great illumination, but enabled photos to be taken providing they were taken at low level — you couldn't take them above 1,000ft with any certainty of success. It turned out to be a hairy business, flying straight and level under 1,000ft, and we got a lot of flak directed our way and lost quite a lot of aeroplanes. Nevertheless, it did a good job, and the army was always pleased with the information we obtained.

'The versatility of the aircraft — and their crews — was demonstrated in several ways. For example, towards the end of the war we were a bit fed up with not being offensive, and got permission to carry bombs instead of flares when we had a moonlight night, when we could see the ground without the use of flares. On these occasions we carried a load of 250lb HE bombs and dropped these on anything which looked interesting — which added a bit to the excitement. They were very short trips, being purely tactical, with the average being about one hour and 20 minutes, but each crew would often fly two or three such trips each night. Being tactical meant, or course, that we moved forward with the army from Normandy to Amiens, Brussels, Melsbroek, and finally Eindhoven in Holland, so it was easy to carry out up to three sorties each night, being so close to the front line at all times.

'Then, early in 1945, a threat from German midget submarines presented itself off the Belgian and Dutch coasts, and yet again the Wellington demon-

Above: 'M-Mike' lands 'too low' on Hal Far, Malta . . .
J. Oldacre

strated its ubiquity. One flight of the squadron had their aircraft modified to carry depth charges, and were deployed to the small airfield at Knokke on the Belgian coast. Here they carried out anti-submarine patrols — just like old times in the Mediterranean!

'The Wellington's ability to absorb punishment in terms of enemy fire was most welcome, and confirmed over and over again. Many Wimpys came back quite badly shot up but still flying — though I must add that losses were fairly high. But even the tough old Wimpy couldn't stand up to the concentrated punishment we received on the ground at Melsbroek on 1 January 1945, when the Luftwaffe had its final fling. They burned beautifully! However, we were fully re-equipped within 48 hours with new aircraft — a quite remarkable achievement. To the best of my belief, No 69 Squadron was the only squadron to be operating Wellingtons right up to VE-Day (in Europe), so I suppose it can be said that the Wimpy, along with the Spitfire, was one of very few British aircraft to operate right throughout the war.'

Left: Quarry-hunting on Malta — literally!   *G. S. Leslie*

Centre left: On a sandy beach in Egypt . . .

Bottom left: Wimpy XIII of 69 Sqn over English countryside, June 1944.
Grp Capt M. Shaw

Right: Mike Shaw with his adjutant, flight commanders and gunnery Leader, 69 Sqn, Melsbroek, early 1945.
Grp Capt M. Shaw

Below: Wellington victims of the Luftwaffe's *Bodenplatte* strafe on Melsbroek, 69 Sqn, 1 January 1945.
Grp Capt M. Shaw

Ginger's Tale

'Ginger' — Jim Ware, DFM — was a rear gunner in Wellingtons, who flew more than 80 operational sorties before his ultimate, near-fatal trip. A born Cockney, he was 25 years old on the morning that Neville Chamberlain told the British population that '... this country is now at war with Germany' and, still recovering from the previous night's celebrations — or in his own phrase, 'Pissed and patriotic' — he immediately went to the nearest recruiting centre and volunteered for RAF aircrew duties. He was accepted for 'straight AG' — air gunner without the normal accompanying wireless training — and after initial training joined No 99 Squadron at Rowley Mile Racecourse, Newmarket, in March 1940:

'It was there that I was crewed up and my skipper was Sgt Jack Hatton who spent some weeks knocking us into shape. He was a grand chap and by the

Below: 'Ginger' Ware (left) and another 99 Sqn AG at Newmarket, Sgt Gardiner, 1941. *N. Didwell*

time I met him he'd already done a few ops. By the time we were ready as a crew for ops I'd realised what a wonderful aircraft the Wellington was. I suppose it was underpowered, but it was tough, strong, and somehow I always felt safe in it. I learned later in my career as an AG that it could stand a hell of a lot of punishment and, providing you still had one engine going, it would get you home. In a way I fell in love with the Wimpy, if it is at all possible for a man to love a machine — I guess other Wimpy men might understand what I mean.

'My first real op was on 10 May 1940 when we were detailed to attack an aerodrome in Holland. It was a short trip and uneventful, though I can remember on the way back seeing the huge fires in Rotterdam; a sight which made me realise that all this was no game, but the real thing. We were kept very busy during this period, and on 29 May we were detailed to bomb a target in France. That day our regular skipper was ill, and we had a young pilot officer take us over. All was well, and we'd bombed the target despite a fair amount of flak, and had no troubles until we got back to England. Here we found the whole country covered with fog. We went from 'drome to 'drome but couldn't land anywhere, and eventually ran out of fuel. We had no alternative but to bale out — I was never so frightened in my life before. I remember after I'd gone out that I looked *down* and saw our Wimpy, and only then realised I was falling upside down. I pulled the ripcord and — to my great relief — the 'chute opened and all seemed so quiet. I heard the Wimpy crash on my way down, but was feeling great because I'd got away with it. What I didn't know at that time was that three other aircraft from our squadron were in the same predicament, and all their crews had to bale out. I'd no idea where I was when I hit the deck — I'd landed in a field, but couldn't see a thing. After a cigarette, I started to walk, and after what seemed ages I heard voices and was then picked up by some chaps in army uniform (probably LDV blokes).

'At that period everybody was thinking about invasion and these chaps thought I was a German parachutist — I don't know who was more frightened, them or me! The officer in charge asked for my identity card, and when I told him I had nothing on me to prove who I was, I was promptly locked up in a hut until early morning, when I was rescued by a squadron leader who told them he'd been looking for us all night. It was then I learned that four crews had baled out that night, and also learned that my pilot had stayed in the Wimpy and crash-landed it at Honington. Twenty-three chaps from 99 Squadron baled out, but only 22 made it; one pilot was killed by jumping too low. It had been my seventh trip — the war was getting dangerous.

'I did 17 trips with Jack Hatton, after which he was posted to an OTU and our second pilot took over. Trips were getting longer now — Berlin, Munich, Hamburg, Kiel, Wilhelmshaven, etc — but our dear old Wimpy, despite taking a beating at times, always got us back. By September 1940 I'd finished my first tour of ops and the crew split up, mostly going to OTUs as instructors. I didn't want to be an instructor so, after a spot of leave, stayed with the squadron as a ''spare'' AG for ops. On getting back from leave I hardly knew any of the chaps; during my three weeks' absence many of my mates had been shot down or posted elsewhere, so I didn't have a regular crew, but flew with any crew needing a rear gunner.

'It was on one such trip, on 16 January 1941, that I was asked to stand in for a gunner who'd gone sick. I didn't know the crew, while they assumed I was new to the squadron and therefore promised to look after me — they'd only been with 99 for about three weeks! The target was Wilhelmshaven and off we went — a long trip over the sea, with little for me to do except to keep a lookout for fighters. We received the usual attentions of the flak boys, dropped our bombs on target, and away home. I was cold and looking forward to my ops' bacon and beans when we got back, when I heard the navigator and pilot arguing as to where we were. The nav said we were over Lincolnshire, but the pilot thought somewhere else. I was thinking to myself ''Make up your bloody minds!'' . . . I then realised we really were lost, and suddenly saw some balloons. I immediately thought. ''We're over London'', then told the pilot about the barrage balloons below. There followed real panic! To cut a long story short, the pilot spotted an

Below : Aircrew billets for 99 Sqn — the race-stand at Newmarket, 1940. From left: Bill Shankland (rear AG in Jack Hatton's crew), Jim 'Ginger' Ware, and Quibell. *J. Ware*

aerodrome shortly after, a small one, made a couple of attempts at landing, and finally made it, running off the 'drome and finishing up in some trees, minus a wing, but collecting bruises all round.

'The aerodrome was Kenley, a tiny fighter station near Croydon. Once again I'd got away with it, but my troubles on this trip were not quite over. Next morning we collected our gear from the wreck, and we were taken to London, to Liverpool Street Station for a train back to Newmarket. Just as we were offloading our stuff at the station from the lorry, something whacked me on the back of the head, and a voice screamed, "German bastard!" It was some dotty old girl clouting me with her umbrella! We were still in flying gear, so she thought we must be Germans.

'By then I felt I must get myself a regular crew; I was fed up with being reserve man for other crews, so I managed to join up with Pilot Officer H. "Robin" Grant as a regular gunner. A few weeks later the squadron left Newmarket and moved to Waterbeach; a new aerodrome where we had proper rooms, baths, showers, a decent Mess, and what's more WAAFs (which made life more interesting...). It was like changing from a doss house to a first-class hotel for 99's boys.'

In January 1942, No 99 Squadron left the UK for India. Grant and Ware organised a scratch crew and proceeded to fly out with the squadron to the Middle East, but were 'tumbled' there and attached to Shallufa, where they kicked their heels for a while, 'organised' themselves on to No 40 Squadron (Wellingtons), and got back on ops again with this unit. Flying against such targets as Benghazi, Tobruk and Derna, Ginger ran up a further 17 or 18 sorties. Then, on 7 August 1942, his luck finally ran out. The target was Tobruk, and the crew of Wimpy 'O-Orange' comprised Flt Lt Robin Grant (pilot), Sgt H. 'Jock' Whyte (second pilot), Plt Off John Hull (observer-nav), Sgt A. 'Arfer' Dunn (W/Op), Sgt 'Chuck' Dauphin (front AG), and Ginger Ware in his customary rear gun turret:

'I woke up that morning with a funny (peculiar) feeling that something was going to happen that day, and that things weren't quite right. I had a cup of tea with my crew and was very quiet, which was not my usual style.

Left: Wellington crew of 99 Sqn at Newmarket, 1940 prior to a daylight sortie to Brest. From left: Alf Walker, Jock Sutherland, Bill Shanklin, Ginger Ware, and an unidentified member. *N. Didwell*

Centre left: Another 99 Sqn crew, 1940. From left; LAC Bill Wynn (W/Op), Sgt (later, Grp Capt) 'Gerry' Blacklock, Sgt Cunningham (Obs), Bill Williams, Cpl Norman Didwell (AG). Wynn was the W/Op on the Wellington taking Air Cdre O. T. Boyd to the Middle East which was forced down in Sicily; while Williams was later killed in a flying accident at Moreton-in-the-Marsh OTU. Gerry Blacklock eventually retired as Group Captain, DSO, OBE, DFC, DFM. *N. Didwell*

Bottom left: Pilot Officer W. M. Dixon receiving congratulations from his 99 Sqn crew on his DFC award in May 1941; a decoration earned from a low-level strafe of Brest harbour in the previous month.

Above right: Wimpy 'L-London' of 99 Sqn, a 250lb GP bomb and friends, the latter including Fg Off Powell, Sgt McIntyre (Wop/AG), Sgt Drury (pilot), and Sgt 'Ginger' Ware, DFM at far right. *N. Didwell*

Some mail arrived from the UK that morning. The rest or the crew got letters, but none for me, which didn't help the mood I was in. I went out to the aircraft, checked my guns and turret; everything was OK. I began to think what a bloody fool I was. My skipper asked me if I was OK. I was rather short with him, saying I was, so he left me to get on with it. We were on that night and the target Tobruk, which we'd been to before and therefore knew what to expect.

'Our journey to the target was uneventful until we reached the target area where we got the usual hot reception with plenty of flak, and for a while were coned in searchlights. The skipper, with a lot of evasive action, managed to get away from the searchlights, we bombed the target area, and set course for home. By then I was feeling ashamed of myself for the mood I'd been in all day, and was beginning to feel like my old self again. We had been on our way back for about three-quarters of an hour or so when Johnny asked me to take a drift for him. He threw out a marker and I got my gun sight on to it and took the drift for him — I'll always remember it read five degrees starboard. I looked up from reading it, to tell him the figure, when to my horror I saw another Wimpy right on top of us, coming from the port quarter! There was no time even to shout to the pilot before he hit us, there was a terrible crash, and I saw him go down in flames.

'I was stunned — I think I must have banged my head — and just sat there unable to move. The warning light on my turret flashed, telling me to bale out. I pulled myself together and became conscious of a horrible silence I could hear no engines. I put my manual handle into gear to turn the turret to the beam but it would only go part-way round, so I got out into the fuselage to escape by the rear escape hatch. Though all this seemed like ages to me, it could only have been a matter of a few seconds. I kicked out the escape hatch with my left leg and was just about to go out when we hit the ground. As we careered along the deck I knew I was hitting my leg but for the moment it didn't hurt. We finally stopped and, somehow, I was outside the aircraft. I've still no idea how this came about, but I'd alway been frightened of fire and possibly it was that fear that got me clear. I noticed the landing lights were on and gave a shout. Robin answered me and found me, and I realised he'd stayed in the aircraft and made a pretty good crash-landing.

'I knew I'd hurt my leg pretty badly, so Robin got the first aid kit and I injected myself in the thigh with a dose of morphine, then, after a cigarette, dozed off. Next morning we had a good look at my leg — and it frightened the life out of me! There wasn't much of my foot left, and the lower part was smashed right up; all we could see were pieces of bone. There was little we could do about it except rip a parachute up and put a rough bandage round it. At least this hid the grisly mess from us. Some time later Jock found us and told us that he'd found "Arfer", who had broken a leg and had his face burnt, being unable to see properly. Both of them left me and fetched "Arfer" back to where I was. They later found Johnny's body — his 'chute hadn't opened properly because he'd jumped too low. We never saw Chuck again.* After Robin and Jock had made "Arfer" and myself as comfortable as possible in the circumstances, it was decided that both pilots would go and seek help for both of us. Jock was a damned good navigator and had worked out our position roughly. They both decided to go because they felt that then at least one of them would get to the German lines — we were too far from our own lines. We agreed on this plan, and about mid-day on the Saturday (8th) they set off. I watched them as far as I could and when they disappeared I felt very miserable and alone.

'By that time my leg was beginning to hurt like hell, and I knew poor "Arfer" was in great pain too. I felt helpless as there was literally nothing either of us could do except wait and hope for the best. As the day wore on I began thinking all sorts of things; wondering how Robin and Jack were getting on — of my parents — then it dawned on me that we'd crashed on my young sister's birthday. I could imagine them all at home being over

the local, supping it up and enjoying themselves, unaware of what was happening to me. Then I pulled myself together smartly — thinking of such things would only send me starkers. Sunday came and went, and by Monday morning — 10 August — "Arfer" and I were both in a pretty bad way. I knew that if help didn't arrive soon we'd both die, yet strangely, I was not frightened about this; in fact I think I'd have welcomed death at this stage as I was in terrible pain. Then I thought of Robin and Jock walking miles across the desert to try and save us both — it wouldn't be fair to them to just give it up now.

'Around noon on the Monday I heard what I thought was the sound of aircraft engines, but felt I must be imagining them. As I searched the sky I saw them, two of them, Fieseler Storch light aircraft. They landed near us and I could see they were German Red Cross planes. A doctor was with them, and they told us that this was their third search for us that day — and would have been the last. Robin and Jock had got through — we owed them our lives. We then learned that they'd been picked up the evening before by an aeroplane, and I was also told later by a German officer that Robin and Jock, at one time, walked through two German minefields and never knew it! The Germans tried to bury Johnny, then put "Arfer" in one aircraft and me in the other. They took us first to Mersa Matruh, but kept us apart, then after a few days I was flown to Athens, where I had my leg amputated.'

*Jock told me after the war that Chuck wandered about for quite a time before being picked up by some Italians.

Prangs

Right: Wellington burning in Crete, 1941, *via S. Howe*

Below: Wellington shot down by flak during a 'Nickel' paper-raid on 23 March 1940, near Eifel.

73

Right: Remains of Wellington T2963 of 115 Sqn which ran out of fuel and crashed into some council houses at Debach, Norfolk in the early morning of 24 June 1941. Two crew members were seriously injured, two slightly injured, and one was unhurt. *S. Evans*

Left: General Sikorski inspecting Wimpy R1697, *'Sonia'* of 304 (Polish) Sqn at Syerston, 1941. *W. Baguley*

Below left: R3295, SR-P, of 101 Sqn shot down at Schienmonnihoog, Holland on 30 November 1941, killing four crew members.
via B. Rijnhout

Below: Wellington T2990, KX-T, of 311 (Czech) Sqn going down in flames to the guns of the German nightfighter ace, Major Prinz zur Lippe Weissenfeld on the night of 22 June 1941. *B. Rijnhout*

74

Above: Bent Wimpy at LG 09,
North Africa, 1942

Right: Wellington graveyard in
Libya, 1942.

Below: R1804 after a collision
with a steam roller at East
Wretham on 19 July 1941; a
311 (Czech) Sqn aircraft.
B. Rijnhout

Above: K-Kitty, R1090, ED-K of 21 OTU Moreton-in-the-Marsh.

Right: A-Apple (T2703) of 15 Sqn, shot down on the night of 31 March/1 April 1941 in Holland.   *G. Zylstva Collection*

Below: Another 115 Sqn victim, X9873, KO-P, brought down near Schiermonnihoog, Holland.   *B. Rijnhout*

Right: The *Werkhalle* at Rechlin, with its collection of shot down Allied aircraft. Visible aircraft include L7788, KX-E of 311 Sqn and T2703, LS-A of 15 Sqn.   *B. Rijnhout*

Centre right: A 205 Group Wellington, possibly a 150 Sqn machine (?), from Foggia, Italy, which raided the Manfried Weiss factory in Budapest on 3 April 1944. This aircraft, piloted by an Australian, Flt Sgt Gordon Pemberton, who was severely wounded, was ditched in the Keszthely Bay of Lake Balaton. By staying at his controls Pemberton saved the lives of his crew, but died himself, being buried in the nearby cemetery.   *L. Tabori*

Below: A Wellington T10 after a fiery crash-landing.

Sun, Sand and Stars

Although the Wellington acquired a doughty reputation on operations over Europe, from the first day of the war, by mid-1943 its bomber role against Germany had been taken over by the newer, four-engined heavies, such as the Lancaster and Halifax, and the ultimate (officially) bombing sorties were flown by Wimpys of No 300 (Polish) Squadron against Hanover on the night of 8 October 1943; the close of four year's sustained operations by the Wimpy in this context. However, in September 1940, No 70 Squadron — based then at Kabrit, Egypt with Vickers Valentia biplane bombers — began re-equipment with Wimpys, and on 18/19 September the first Wimpy operations were flown; including a raid on Benghazi harbour which inaugurated the famed 'Mail Run' to that priority target by all subsequent Wimpy units. In November 1940, Nos 37 and 38 Squadrons arrived in Egypt to complement 70's Wimpys, and further Wellington units were formed or re-equipped in the Middle East zone over the following two years. And despite the later provision of long-range designs such as the Liberator, Middle East Wellingtons were to continue on firstline operations until early 1945.

N. E. McIntyre was a sergeant observer when he first joined 37 Squadron at Feltwell in August 1940, and was to remain with the squadron until September 1941 when, having completed his tour of ops, he returned to the UK:

'My initial crew — captain, Sgt D. Beddow — did 12 ops over France and Germany, ranging from "makee-learners" on the ports holding barges for the intended German invasion to targets in the Ruhr, Leipzig and Kiel. Navigational aids were conspicuous by their absence, and it was DR (Dead Reckoning) coupled with pinpoints when visibility was good which brought us on to target areas.

Incidentally, "Willy" Merton (Wg Cdr W. Merton, OC, later ACM Sir Walter) impressed upon us at each briefing the necessity of doing a three-course wind-check over target areas for a correct wind-setting on the bomb sight. This meant flying three straight-and-level courses for a few minutes, usually with plentiful flak to contend with — it can be left to imagination what captains and navigators thought of such a scheme!

'Sergeant Beddow completed his first tour in November 1940, and I joined another crew, with Sgt R. T. Spiller as captain, and the squadron was posted to Middle East Command, some aircraft stopping over at Malta to boost the efforts against the Italians. The squadron flew individually at intervals to Malta, via Worthing, Marseilles and Bizerta to Luqa. We made a landfall at Bizerta at about 9,000ft at approximately 0700hrs, to be greeted by a fair amount of friendly French flak thrown at us, and as we scuttled away an Italian Macchi 200 jumped us. We dived to sea level and eventually shook him off, with the assistance of our phlegmatic New Zealander rear gunner and his Brownings, but not before collecting a few hits, one of them peppering the backside of an unfortunate armourer travelling with us. We made Luqa at 0900hrs and the armourer survived after a few days in sick bay, despite initial bleeding. Whilst at Malta we flew sorties against Brindisi and Valona, Albania. This latter I particularly remember because of the severe thunderstorms we met over the Balkan coast, preventing location of both primary and secondary targets, and with the DR plot ending up like a spider's web due to the numerous changes of course we had to make.

'We left Malta on 20 December and flew to Shallufa in the Suez Canal zone, which became our main base for the remainder of our Middle East tour.

Targets from there included Benghazi, Tobruk, Derna along the northern coast, and Rhodes and Karpathos in the Dodecanese. From Shallufa we enjoyed two detachments to Greece and one to Iraq. Operating from Menidi, near Athens and Paramythia, a landing ground in from the west coast towards Corfu, I recall two sorties from Paramythia ("Valley of the Fairies"). On 20 February 1941, in company with another Wimpy (Flt Lt M. Baird-Smith), we dropped bales of bread and bully-beef to the Greek Army at Kelcyre inside the Albanian border. We made it as low-level as possible, and could almost see the joy on the faces of the men below as they scampered through the snow to the drops. On 16 March Intelligence learned that Mussolini was due in Tirana, the Albanian capital; we hoped that our bombs more than shook him in the royal palace.

'The Boche was by then coming down through the Balkans and we finished our stay in Greece with a raid on the Sofia railway yards, Calatos aerodrome on Rhodes, and German transport concentrations coming south through Ptolemais, Kozene and Florina. I well remember that last op. The CO (Wg Cdr R. M. Collard) decided to skipper the aircraft and, after bombing and strafing the German transports on the road through the three locations, the weather closed in on us and, with Mount Olympus (9,500ft) quite handy, we climbed in as tight a spiral as we dared, eventually breaking cloud, heading east, and (with a sigh of relief) pinpointed the three-fingered peninsula south-east from Salonika. This was on 16 April, and three days later we packed our bags and bade farewell to Greece, now being invaded by the Germans. Just after leaving Athens Ken Bevan, our Kiwi rear gunner, reported a fighter chasing us. We dropped to sea-level and, with his customary cool commentary and marksmanship, he persuaded the Messerschmitt to break off.

'A detachment to Iraq from 1-12 May gave us our first opportunity to be angry during daylight. Based at Shaibah, we flew "security patrols" over Habbaniyah and bombed "Raschid aerodrome" and the military installations and 'drome at Mosul. In addition to bombs we dropped "meaningful" messages to one Raschid Ali, the villain of the piece. On return to

Shallufa, Vic Slater and myself volunteered for ACP duties in the "Blue" at Fuka satellite aerodrome, where we spent just over three weeks gradually becoming proficient in dousing goose-neck flares before the Boche came over, and relighting them in time for our aircraft to land. Then on 26 August we returned to Shallufa, and three weeks later left the Middle East for the UK by sea, via Durban and the Cape.'

Chas Hughes was a Wop/AG, trained at No 1 Signals School, Cranwell, and the gunnery school at Evanton. He next went to 15 OTU, Harwell but was 'detached' to Harwell's satellite at Hampstead Norris in early 1942, at the time of the famous Harris 'Thousand-bomber' raids, where he was commissioned as a Pilot Officer:

'The 1,000-raids produced lots of panic, with all hands to the wheel to spread that horrid brown de-icing paste over wing leading edges, spinners, etc. Then to the briefing where we were told that everybody must bomb from 14,000ft — a joke! It should perhaps be well recorded that Wellington III, HX876, "O-Orange" actually bombed Bremen from 6,500ft — and was hanging on its props at that! My skipper then was Plt Off Brian Hunter, a bank clerk from Hull who was later to lose a leg when he hit a bowser landing at Malta in early 1943; while my second pilot was Plt Off Clem

Below: In the shadow of Gibraltar's famous Rock, X9889 of 40 Sqn, in late 1941. *IWM*

Above: Mk XIII Wellington, MP707 (nearest) in Egypt, circa 1942. *IWM*

Fowler, a London lad who later flew Beaufighters.

'After the OTU "sessions" we were off to Portreath in Cornwall to collect a brand-new Wimpy III fitted with torpedo-dropping gear, "P-Peter", then off to Gibraltar. Our call-sign was "Tablet, P-Peter" and Gibraltar was "Sermon", and I'd been calling and calling on the R/T to no avail, when Brian overshot after touching down and we nearly ended up in the sea. As we climbed hurriedly away a voice from below finally piped up saying, "Hello Tablet P-Peter. Are you in trouble?". My retort was, "No, nothing that a bit of finger-extraction on the deck can't solve!" We stayed at Gib until the following evening when, with two wing-tanks on the rest bed and cylinder tanks in the bomb bay, we took off with instructions to fly to LG224, 26km from Cairo, and to be sure to be east of 30-degrees east by daylight because of a German fighter base at Pontalaria — we were! Fourteen hours and 35 minutes later we arrived at LG224 near Cairo, where I removed my jacket and hung it on the tent pole, only to find when retrieving the jacket a few minutes later that my wallet had been stolen. Though formally charged with "losing my paybook in an active theatre of operations", the bit that really hurt was the loss of £20 in cash, which I couldn't report because we were officially only allowed to take £5 out of the UK!

'On to Almaza, and then to 148 Squadron at Kabrit on the Great Bitter Lake, where we left "P-Peter" and never saw her again. All we had on the squadron were clapped-out Mk 1as. Using the same airfield at that time were Nos 40, 70, 104 and 108 Squadrons. Owing to the lack of space in the accommodation, my navigator, Sgt John Chandler, and I slept under a verandah in the open on charpoy-type beds, with each of the four legs standing in basins of creosote to stop bugs and "beasties" crawling up the legs into the beds. We weren't placed on the battle order on the first night, but a crew with a sick navigator borrowed ours. I turned in before the scheduled 10pm take-off, and when I woke next morning I turned to look at my nav's bed but it was empty. On enquiry, a corporal simply pointed to Wimpy "V-Victory" in the lake with its tail in the air. It had gone straight in on take-off and my nav was killed. We buried him at Geneifa.

'We moved from Kabrit and went up "into the Blue" to a strip known as Kilo 40 on the Cairo-Alexandria road, and on 23 October when El Alamein broke we moved up to LG 106 at El Daba to give the Eighth Army support. One morning at LG 106 I woke to find a Wimpy barely 50 yards from my tent, shot up on its belly. It had arrived during the night, yet I hadn't heard a thing. The next few weeks were hectic when we flew close support sorties against enemy transports etc to help the army move faster. Each op took about 2½-3hrs, and we had to do two ops each night to make them count as one operation. Just prior to El Alamein we did nearly all our sorties to Tobruk or Benghazi, bombing shipping, with occasional odd trips to targets like

Mersa Matruh. With us then was a pilot called Charlie Klimkie, who had a delayed take-off one night and was therefore told to stooge around the desert for something to bomb. He spotted a light below and decided to hit it with four 1,000lb bombs. It was a German ammo train outside Mersa Matruh station and Charlie hit it from about 1,000ft — and very nearly went up with it.

'We next moved to LG 67 on top of an escarpment 30 miles south of Bardia. Whoever chose this site must have been around the twist, because it was one hell of a job for the lads to get petrol and water bowsers up to us. My last raid in the desert was an easy one. Having rendered Heraklion airfield on Crete unserviceable, we used El Adem as an advance base for a raid on Crete's other airfield, known as Casteli Peliadi. On landing at El Adem we burst a tail wheel, and toil as they might the ground crew couldn't remove the wheel. Came darkness and they gave up, and we slept under the wing. Next morning the erks tried again and Geronimo! — it came off at the first turn of the spanner. After much bad language we set off to take the bombs back to base. Shortly after we handed over our few remaining Wimpys to 40 Squadron and went back to Cairo by road, and from there, by devious forms of transport, sea, road and air, I returned to the UK.'

Jim Sterrett was a bomb-aimer, initially trained in South Africa, whose introduction to Wellingtons came in July 1944, at 77 OTU, Qastina in Palestine, and who subsequently flew the type on operations with No 104 Squadron:

'We had crewed-up en route to the OTU except for a "Drivers, airframe" and when the posting of pilots arrived we all agreed that we didn't want any gong-hunting sprog pilot officer, but rather a mature type who looked as though he had a wife and family he'd wish to see again. Thus, our eventual choice, Doug Skinner, was snapped up because he then had prematurely iron-grey hair! Our first confirmation that the Wimpy was a good, tough aeroplane came on 18 July 1944 on our first cross-country exercise. Over Baltim the starboard engine blew a cylinder head and lost some of its cowling. We were ordered to standby for a bale-out. As the bomb-aimer I would have been the first to go and, looking down through the open hatch waiting for the dreaded order "Go", I remember I thought "Why now? We haven't even been on ops yet". After some colourful language over the intercomm, the two drivers thought they

Below: Wimpys of 205 Group awaiting their bomb-loads, Egypt, circa 1942. *IWM*

might be able to feather the engine and hold the kite steady for a while, so we set course for El Ballah, a gunnery school, were we landed safely with one very overheated engine. We all got out, went on our knees in the sand, and gave heartfelt thanks to Allah . . .

'Eight days later we set out on a cross-country to Cyprus, where we carried out the usual exercises — photography, bombing, gunnery, etc. On the way back Charlie Williams, our rear gunner, noticed that the bomb doors were still open. A certain amount of hand-pumping followed, but we were forced to make a flapless approach. The undercarriage collapsed and bits of propellers flew off. The runway burst through the hatch and belly and the inside of the aircraft was full of dust and debris; yet Doug managed to hold her steady. Following the normal drill, I exited through the top hatch on to the wing and, very conscious of a sizzling sound from the hot engines, completed my first-ever 100 yards in even time! Charlie had banged his head against his Brownings and was dazed. He got out of his turret, dripping blood, and not realising it was so high in the air due to the posture of the aircraft . . . it again proved to us how robust the Wimpy was. Doug was torn off a strip next day by the CFI, but then a fault in the hydraulic system was discovered. The kite was a write-off.

'My first op with 104 Squadron, from Foggia, Italy, was on 17 October 1944 as bomb-aimer to Sgt Parks' crew, his usual bomb-aimer being ''unserviceable''. We flew in Wellington X, LP549 and the target was Vinkovci's marshalling yards. Enemy aircraft were sighted but the TIs (target indicators) were late, so we had

Above: 'The Jeep', 'W' of 70 Sqn, which was eventually shot down in flames over Derna, North Africa on 11 November 1942.
G. E. Wilson

Left: Mail-Run pioneers. A trio of 37 Sqn's Wimpys, May 1941. Nearest is T2875.

Right: Landing victim at LG 09, Middle East.

to go round again; NOT a popular decision, particularly coming from a sprog bomb-aimer! We had a good run-up and dropped nine 500lb and nine 250lb GPs. On 21 October I again flew with Sgt Park in "R-Robert" to bomb Maribor marshalling yards with six SBCs of incendiaries and three 500lb GPs. There was the usual flak and a sight of the ground battle, while enemy aircraft were reported, and weather was bad over the target. Checking the bomb bay on the way back I noticed that two or three 500lb GPs were still with us; the news was not well received. After going through all the normal drills without any success, it was decided that I chop up the floor so that I could effect manual release. One bomb we did, the other(s) landed with us... Park greased the Wimpy in VERY gently..! The ground crew were very annoyed about the state of the floor, but at least I'd missed the hydraulic pipes due to careful axe-work.

'Our first op as a complete crew came on 17 November 1944 in Wimpy 515 "Y" — a raid against troop concentrations and transport at South Jenica/Novi Pazar, but we were recalled to base after sighting the enemy coastline, and jettisoned 18 × 250lb bombs in the Adriatic. We went back again next day in daylight and dropped three sticks of 250-pounders on some MT. Subsequent sorties included attacks on a bridge and troops at Podgorica, more troop concentrations at Rogatica, a supply drop to Predgrad — this one on 2 December when the DZ was covered in 10-10ths cloud and we had to bring our goodies back — and a similar drop next day to Berane, where the DZ was again obscured by cloud, but we released the load on a Gee fix. On 15 December we were in "P-Peter" but were told to stand down. We were all ready to dive off to Foggia when we were told that ops were "on" again. Our original wireless operator suddenly went "special sick" — he was eventually graded LMF — and we flew with a spare bod. We took off with a load of 18 × 250lb GPs to bomb MT and troops north of the town of Klopot, and it turned out to be a decidedly uncomfortable trip because soon after take-off the escape hatch above the cockpit blew open. We spent much of the time and energy trying to close it, even with the aid of sideslipping, but with no success. Charlie was brought forward from his rear turret to help — being the strong one — and he was nearly sucked out of his flying boots. However, because it was the skipper's birthday, we had to press on. We had no flying goggles with us and eyes became very sore after hours in the howling draught. We met some light flak, but we got some MT fires going and stoked up others a bit. Next day was spent just bathing our sore eyes.

'More sorties against troop concentrations and transports followed, then on Christmas Eve a general stand-down was declared, except for crews who drew straws for ops on Christmas Day — our crew drawing one straw. That evening I won a bottle of White Label in the mess draw, together with a chicken, cigarettes, chocolate, etc; all of which were shared out in a tent party which ended early — at 0100hrs! Next day — Christmas Day — we took off at mid-day for a supply drop to Crnomelj, near Predgrad; a straightforward trip with a good drop, and coming home on a wireless homing to a belated Christmas dinner which we were too clapped out to enjoy. Yet more supply and bombing trips followed. The weather was bloody cold; indeed, a supply drop to Circhina on 8 January in "V" had to be aborted because of icing up to 11,000ft which built up on the wing leading edge faster than I'd ever seen. As our skipper said of this trip later, "It was the most frightening experience of instrument flying, instruments at loggerheads, speed falling off when the altimeter was unwinding in descent off the clock, then speed shooting up again when the altimeter was winding up".

'On 20 January 1945, in "W", we dropped our first 4,000lb Cookie, from 8,500ft over Odine marshalling yards. We'd arrived a little early and got some flak before finally dropping. Then came a spot of leave in Sorrento — running water and sheets on the bed — sheer luxury! *La Boheme* from Box 22 in the San Carlo and other touches of a forgotten civilised way of life, followed — back at Foggia a few days later — by the Anglo-Polish Ballet company performing *Les Sylphides* etc. Then back to work on 8 February when we bombed Verona; a good trip against the usual opposition, but a long wait on the circuit afterwards for the "green", and an overshoot after first touchdown. Fiume in daylight followed on the 15th where we dropped our load on the oil refinery and harbour installations; a trip where I was distinctly put off by the box barrage being clearly seen into which we'd have to go during our approach — it had never seemed so bad at night. On 20 February we

dropped our second Cookie, on Udine marshalling yards; then on 24 February 1945 came my last trip in a Wimpy. We went to Brescia to drop two 2,000lb HC bombs on the marshalling yards there. It was a good trip, though the flak was accurate and we brought some back with us, and plenty of fighter activity. The grapevine said that Mussolini was giving the locals a pep talk at the time, so we liked the idea of setting off the Eyetie air raid sirens. After de-briefing the CO informed us we were tour-expired.'

Art Wahlroth, a Canadian, was trained on Whitleys on his OTU, then promptly posted to Wellington IIs with No 405 Squadron RCAF at Driffield and Pocklington for operations. He next instructed on Wimpy 1cs at Wellesborne Mountford and Moreton-in-the-Marsh, before returning to ops with No 37 Squadron, 1943-44 on

EXTRACT :- D.R.O's DATED 14
R.A.F. STATION, TA-KALI, M

A GIBBET HAS BEEN ERE
ON THE CORNER OF THE ROAD
LEADING TO THE CAVES. AN
MAN, WOMAN OR CHILD, CIVIL
OR SERVICE PERSONNEL, FO
GUILTY OF SABOTAGE, THE
OR IN ANY OTHER WAY IMPE
THE WAR EFFORT AND SUE
SEQUENTLY SHOT, WILL BE
HUNG FROM THIS GIBBET
A WARNING TO ALL OTHE

Top: Z8345 comes to grief in North Africa, 1942; 'S-Sugar' of 104 Sqn
V. Cashmore via D. Vincent

Above: A notice board at Ta Kali, Malta in May 1942 which hardly needs amplification . . . *L. Jordan*

Wellington Xs. His memories of his Middle East tour are not simply of operations, but of incidents and individuals (no names, no pack-drill!) 'I'll always remember . . .

'The officious MO giving us yellow fever shots. We moved to the head of the line, feigning fainting and pain, with loud noises . . . resulting in a jittery line-up.

'The non-dressy chamois gloves issued for the Middle East. We looked at them with disdain . . . until we got there and tried to pick up anything with bare hands.

'The smell of eucalyptus trees in Gibraltar.

' "Pass the oranges" — always heard when a new crew arrived. A tin of ascorbic acid tablets would be passed down the table.

'The ever present sand — one had to blow a channel when writing a letter, for the pen to travel in.

'The ever-blowing desert wind . . . and the tail gunner who left his turret on landing and walked forward, not realising that the engines were still running until he was decapitated (I very nearly caught his head like a football . . .).

'The hung-over rigger who each morning would kick the tyres, sign his DI, and go back to bed. When I first saw this I hit the roof, but was assured that later in the day he would go over the machine thoroughly, and that I'd never have any trouble. They were right; I tried to catch him out for a month by odd tricks like reversing battery terminals, wires, gas cocks etc — and I never had any trouble.

'The squadron MO who gleefully and sadistically painted men blue who were found to have lice. Aircrews escaped this treatment, which wouldn't have helped in any escape situation.

'The obese armament Warrant Officer who *led* the parade of those running away from an unexploded 4,000lb bomb in a crashed aircraft.

'Travelling Arabs, father riding the donkey, mother and kids walking behind. If the area was suspected of having land mines, however, mother and kids walked in front.

'The Group Captain ("Teddy" Beare of 231 Wing) who would scrounge Canadian cigarettes from me . . . and enjoyed the Vees he got in the darkness of the flare-path, thinking they were Sweet Caps.

'The entire crew losing their break-fast when, after several years of RAF rations, we had a wonderful meal at an American hospital, for whom we were doing some ferry work.

'The Scottish dancing in the Mess, to the tune of two chanters, as a means of keeping warm. Visits to the bar between sets increased the tempo . . . and small men were periodically hurled right over the wall.

'The no-face patients at Heliopolis hospital in Cairo, mostly pilots of burnt-out P-40s which stretched in never-ending line across Africa.

'The police in downtown Cairo; one in a white suit on either side of the street in each block, and on each intersection two, in black suits, with shotguns . . . this protection was mainly for us.

'The rains, which turned our airfield into a salt lake. We had to use mud-boards in order to move at all over the resulting gumbo.

'Stripping equipment and draining petrol from aircraft, and moving them from a small, unflooded taxi-strip, flaps down, brakes set, and full bore, to a nearby strip on stony, high ground.

'Yank fighter pilots taxying their P-38s at about 40mph, complete with long peaked caps, sunglasses, and chomping the inevitable cigar.

'The Thunderbolt that rammed one of our Wellingtons at Foggia. It was condemned and in a week was stripped down for spares. Our aircraft, broken in two, was resurrected and flying again in a matter of weeks . . .

'Seeing the tents blow away in a 5am gale, and the semi-clad refugees ultimately gathering into aircraft, which they started up in order to keep warm.

'The Yank officer in Italy, abjectly apologising to his crew chief for the damage to the aeroplane, when he belly-landed his B-17.

'Coming down the Adriatic near dawn, holding height to just brush over the 3,000ft mountain that forms a spur on the boot of Italy, then letting down to the airfield, feeling that we were going down into a hole.

'The crew who let their intercomm go out over the air and, on hearing me report in after a trip, commented loud and clear, "There's that bastard Wahlroth back again". Being the Flight Commander, I ripped off the pilot, one of my former students — for laxity in radio procedure. . .

'The intense activity of Russians, Americans and English alike to shift masonry in an attempt to get my tail gunner out from under a collapsed building... and the subsequent funeral.

'The ENSA shows in the Opera House in Foggia, where troops in the balconies would blow up condoms, letting them float down to where the American nurses sat... at which point one of the nurses would reach up with a lighted cigarette and puncture one; this bringing the house down.

'The San Carlo Opera company in Naples, the opera *Lucia di Lammermoor* with the cast in Highland kilts... and all with baggy-kneed underwear.

'Crossing Italy from Naples to Foggia, across three ranges of mountain peaks, in and out of cloud. Searchlights ringed Foggia, coning at 15,000ft, we let down in a left-hand circuit around and through the reappearing and disappearing beams of light until we broke out, hopefully, in the clear below... a cold sweat was the order of the day.

'The constant relief from tension once we were off and climbing on course in the night sky...'

The Middle East Wimpys' saga of bombing operations was heavily complemented by the aircraft's role as a torpedo-strike vehicle in the unceasing struggle to deprive Rommel's Afrika Korps of essential fuel and other supplies. E. A. Sanders, after training at 15 OTU, Harwell, completed a tour of 35 ops with No 38 Squadron in the Middle East in 1942, was then screened as an instructor on Wimpys back in the UK, and eventually undertook his second ops tour on Halifaxes with 78 Squadron:

'No 38 Squadron co-operated with 221 Squadron, whose Wimpys were fitted with ASV equipment. 221 located any convoy and dropped flares, and we homed in on them and attacked either into the flares or along the moonpath. We had a sort of Heath Robinsonish bomb sight (home-made, I believe) mounted just outside the pilot's windscreen, but it was not often used. Our method was to fly as low on the water as we could, aiming the nose of the aircraft about half the ship-length ahead, and drop the torpedo as near as possible to the target. The best "way out" afterwards used to be over the ship, down on the water again, then a steep turn away. The torpedoes could be released singly or together by the pilot. Incidentally, our practice

torpedo-dropping exercises were carried out on the Great Bitter Lake, and one target I recall was King Farouk's yacht moored at Ismailia!

'No 221 Squadron's Wimpys had a massive array of aerials along the fuselage and were known as "Sticklebacks", and in addition to their ASV equipment they carried a considerable number of parachute flares which they dropped on our request. 221 was usually airborne about an hour before 38 Squadron, to enable them to search for any target convoy. Although we in 38 were based at Shallufa on the Canal, we usually operated from Gianaclis (LG 226) just over an hour's flying from base to the west of Cairo, and torpedoes were flown up there and stocked for operations. Opposition was always intense. For example, on 25 October 1942 we attacked a convoy between Malta and Tobruk consisting of two motor vessels, four destroyers and one escort vessel. We were attacked for some 15 minutes by three Junkers Ju88s escorting the convoy, but our low speed with undercarriages and flaps down enabled us to get away. I remember when our aircraft went up to Palestine (Aqir, if I remember correctly) for modifications, we understood they were coming back with front turrets removed and armour plating installed. In reality they were only replaced with fabric and plywood!

'As for the aircraft itself, I always found the Wimpy a wonderful aeroplane, and I eventually completed some 1,200hrs in the type. At first sight, when standing looking out of the astro-dome, it frightened me to see how the wings moved up and down in flight! I can still recall too the tiring effort of having to pump oil every two hours or so from the reserve tanks. The pump handle was a short affair on the port side on the floor, and it required quite an effort in winter, at height, when the oil was cold.'

In late August 1942, Rommel decided upon his final bid to defeat the Eighth Army in North Africa and thus capture the Egyptian Delta zone, and therefore asked for supplies to be shipped to Tobruk; a decision fraught with risk as it meant bringing Axis supply convoys well within range of the Wimpy torpedo-strike aircraft from their Egyptian bases. One such convoy was spotted on 28 August, steaming west of Crete, with a heavy destroyer escort.

Right: Crew from 104 Sqn, Foggia, Italy on 25 February 1945. From left: Sgts Wilf Eardley (Nav) & Charlie 'Ice-Cool' Williams (R/AG), Flt Sgt Jack Gray (W/Op), Sgt Doug Skinner (Capt), Sgt Jim Sterrett (B/A). Taken in front of Wimpy *'Flak-Happy Harry'* on the day after the crew's last sortie of their tour of ops. *S. J. Sterrett*

Centre right: Wellington *'Flak-Happy Harry'* of 104 Sqn, Foggia, Italy in February 1945. *S. J. Sterrett*

Bottom right: Sgt Doug Skinner, skipper of *'Flak-Happy Harry'* of 104 Sqn at Foggia, Italy in February 1945. This and the previous two views were deliberately taken *after* the end of the crew's ops' tour, due to a superstition about any photos being taken *during* the tour... *S. J. Sterrett*

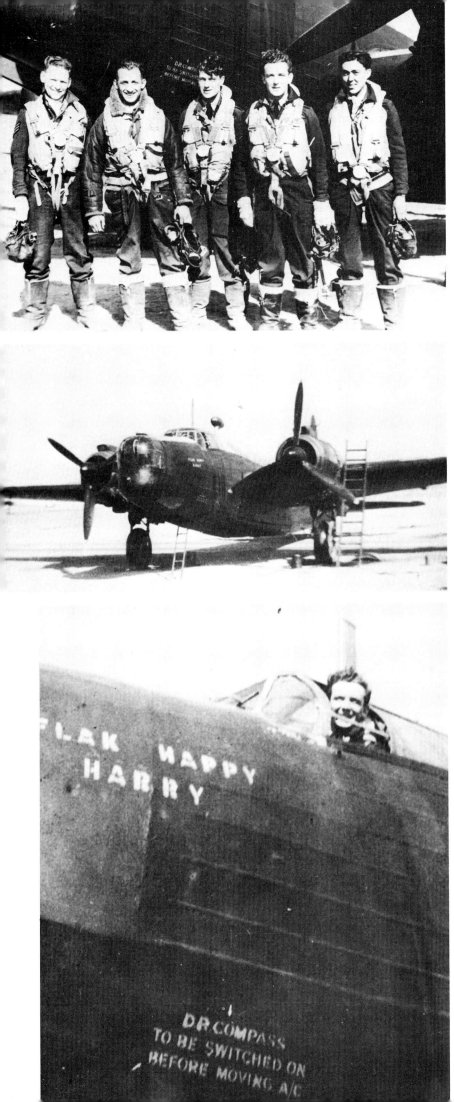

That evening Wellingtons and Liberators set out and attacked the convoy due north of Derna, blowing up one of the two main fuel-carrying store-ships. In the early hours of 29 August a second wave of Wimpy torpedo aircraft took up the assault; one pilot being Flt Lt M. Foulis, DFC of 221 Squadron whose official description of his individual attack reads:

'We sighted the ships at 0015hrs in the moonpath. There was no cloud and a bright moon. We could see the ship clearly, a vessel of about 8,000 tons or perhaps a little less. There was one destroyer about two miles ahead of her, another about a mile on her port bow, and a third close in to her starboard quarter. I spent about 20 minutes flying across the moonpath on the west side to work out my line of attack. Eventually I made up my mind on the best approach and we commenced a long run-up on the ship's starboard bow. She was not fully in the moonpath but she was clearly visible. I could see no white wake astern of her, but the track in the sea along which she travelled could be seen. I dropped my first torpedo at a range of 700yd, and the second at 400yd. We flew ahead of one destroyer but were not fired upon until after the torpedoes had been released. As soon as the second torpedo was gone, I pulled the aircraft up and we passed over between the centre and the stern of the ship.

'The torpedoes were on their way but had not yet reached her. The destroyer close in and the ship herself both opened fire, the latter at point blank range. My rear gunner could not fire at the ship because he could not depress his guns sufficiently. I took violent evasive action and we escaped damage. The navigator, who was in the astrodome, reported two bright orange flashes on the vessel, astern and amidships. I swung the aircraft round and we could all see two great columns of water going up above her masts. It was clear that both torpedoes had hit.

'We ran up and down on the west side watching developments. Very quickly thick grey smoke began to come out of the ship. The destroyers closed in to her, and within five minutes a heavy smoke pall lay over all the ships. We could plainly smell this smoke in the aircraft; it smelt oily and acrid. We sent our first target report: "Two hits on tanker, stationary, smoking". After about ten minutes the smoke cleared and a large oil patch

87

was all that remained of the merchant ship. The destroyers were there but nothing else. We sent another signal ''Tanker believed sunk, large oil patch seen''.'

Acting Squadron Leader M. Foulis, DFC failed to return from a torpedo-strike sortie in Wellington HX487 on 18 April 1943.

If operations predominate the story of any wartime aircraft's career, it should be remembered that the quantitative bulk of any air force's personnel were not engaged solely in flying at the 'sharp end'. Behind the operational crews stretched a long line of men and women whose tasks and unceasing labours supported the firstline efforts. In the context of the Wellington, this theme was especially true for the Wimpy's service outside the UK. Take the wartime career of Peter Powell for merely one example. Awarded his wings and sergeant's chevrons in November 1941, he was eventually commissioned in February 1944, and reached the rank of Flight Lieutenant by late 1945. From July 1942 to August 1945 he served with Nos 1 and 3 Aircraft Delivery Units, and from October 1943 to May 1945 ferried no less than 42 Wimpys to various Middle East units:
'Towards the end of 1943, No 3 ADU (later, No 3 Ferry Unit) was based at Oujda in Morocco, and I had my first

flight in what was to become my favourite kite, the Wimpy. At that time Wellingtons were being flown out from Cornish airfields to Rabat, and we were responsible for taking them on from there to Cairo and Italy. On taking over a Wimpy at Sale (the Rabat airfield), the first thing I did was to check the tyre pressures, and found that these were invariably about 20psi too high; a natural consequence of the difference in temperature between North Africa and the UK. I soon grew to love the Wimpy because one couldn't find a better aircraft for ferrying purposes. It had only one vice — a pre-dictable swing to starboard on take-off which was counter-acted by opening the starboard throttle first and follow-ing this with port throttle when it started to drift to port.

'The ploy for a successful trip to Cairo was to organise a night stop not too far away — El Adem was favourite. An early start next morning ensured the disposal of the aircraft at Cairo West in time to be at the bar of the pub we ferry types used by opening time; necessary because we well knew that there were only ever two barrels of Stella beer available! One of the things we had to watch on a night stop, however, was the guarding of valuable equipment ie the sextant and naviga-tion watches, though the things most likely to vanish unless we took action were thermos flasks.

Above left: Medicine in the field. A 38 Sqn Wimpy crew member with a broken back from a landing crash is treated surgically on the spot by the 'Quack', with the help of a Coles crane . . . *L. Jordan*

Above: Navigator in a Middle East Wellington in his office. *Bippa*

Right: Wellington XIII with ASV II radar stickleback array, possibly a machine from 221 Sqn (?). *IWM.*

'After 30-odd years one tends to mainly remember the good times, and I can still recall one beautiful morning in October 1944 in Wimpy HZ929 when we were making for Gibraltar for Oujda at a height of 5,000ft, when I told my navigator that he could go back to sleep — I could see the Rock when we were still 100 miles away from it. The bad times were invariably connected with bad weather, because in some 400 hours flying in Wimpys I never once had the slightest trouble from the Hercules engines. In lousy weather we became expert in coast-crawling, hundreds of miles following the north and west African coasts with cloud base down to well below 1,000ft. On one occasion in January 1945, in MF298, flying from Sale to Takoradi, we were flying at about 2,000ft — in winter we never went higher than this as it was too cold. My wireless operator, Ted Julian, was keen on flying, so I installed him in the cockpit and then got down to a game of chess with the navigator, Alan Tait. All three of us became so engrossed in what we were doing that we forgot we were running on an overload tank. This soon ran out and both engines cut. Alan and I looked at each other, then simultaneously shot out of our seats like startled rabbits. I heaved up a wing that poor Ted had dropped, while Alan went back to switch tanks.

'One winter trip which was very popular was to ferry Mk XIIIs and XIVs down from Rabat to the coastal squadrons based on the Gold Coast (Ghana). As the major part of this route was over Spanish and Vichy French territories it involved a gigantic coast-crawl, but it was very pleasant to get into KD (Khaki Drill) for a day or two, and get away from the North African winter. On one trip we ran into a line squall after taking off from Freetown, and had no alternative but to fly down the beach, as the base was down at about 100ft and visibility no more than 100yds. We did this for an hour — our only worry being whether any other aircraft was doing the same thing and coming in the opposite direction!

'Our last jobs, early in 1945, were re-equipping the Wimpy squadrons then based in Italy with Liberators. It became quite common to try out two or even three Liberators at Maison Blanche before finding a serviceable kite; yet on landing at Foggia we were presented with fly-back Wellingtons which literally went like sewing machines — a tribute to the Wimpy, and no less a measure of the high quality of maintenance on the squadrons.'

A Lament of Erks

Unpublicised, usually unhonoured, even occasionally unwanted, the Erks — the RAF's universal nickname for all non-commissioned airmen of the ground servicing crews — were (and for that matter, still are) the unshakeable rock foundation of the Service. Steely-eyed fighter and bomber crews may well have cornered the 'market' on glittering awards and lavish public acclaim, yet without loyalty, stoic endurance and unceasing toils of the ground crews, all aircrew would be redundant. Whatever the miracles of the micro-chip and computer, no machine of whatever complexity could (or can) wholly replace the ingrained skills and know-how of the experienced human fitter when aeroplanes are concerned. An Erk's daily life during World War 2 was never a sinecure. Pay was minimal, living conditions varied from the comparative luxury of a peacetime station barrack block to a pup tent, charpoy, and hole in the sand, and an overseas posting could often mean three or four years' separation from families and other loved ones. Working circumstances also varied widely. A hangar shelter from the elements, a dispersal hut improvised from spare wood planks, corrugated iron sheets, or whatever scrounged materials were available, a storm-swept open dispersal subject to the extremes of heat, cold or rain, depending on location.

Working hours — the fetish of the modern trades union shop steward or hierarchy — seldom existed in finite form; the job was top priority, 'keeping 'em flying', no matter *how* long it took. A seven-days' working week was the norm, with a 36- or 48-hours' leave pass a rarity, and actual leave a luxury. A bicycle, however ancient was a prized possession for transportation — cars were luxuries for officers only — while off-duty entertainment often depended solely upon self-improvisation. Indeed, improvisation was the key to much of an Erk's

Below: Winter landscape at the Lossiemouth OTU, 1944. *E. A. Saunders*

existence, whether at work or at play; adhering to the book, particularly in technical matters, was too often impossible due to lack of the proper tools or parts. Such omissions were never permitted to delay essential maintenance; the ubiquitous Erk always managed to find a solution, however crude or temporary the available material might be. The universal motto was *Ubendum, Wemendum*.

The following selected reminiscences by various ex-Erks, in differing circumstances, represent a vast population of the unsung airmen and airwomen whose labours and sacrifices provided the essential springboard for eventual victory in the air war of 1939-45. For every anecdote or experience quoted here, a thousand other Erks could tell a parallel tale.

Bob Watson was a prewar Halton Aircraft Apprentice — a 'Trenchard Brat' — one of that vast army of regular-serving Erks who had committed body and soul to the RAF by 'signing-on' at the tender age of 16 years or slightly younger, and undergoing a three-years' 'sentence' of engineering apprenticeship training at the RAF's No 1 School of Technical Training, Halton, Buckinghamshire, before passing out into the ranks of the Service to complete at least 12 years' 'Man's service':

'I joined as a Fitter II and spent the first year training on engines etc, and then the compound trade was split into Fitter IIE (engines) and IIA (airframes)

— so I became a IIA with no arguments! After leaving Halton as a fully-fledged Fitter IIA, my first posting was to a Mechanical Transport (MT) Maintenance Unit! The Records Office eventually discovered (or admitted) their error and posted me to Henlow which, by January 1940 when I arrived, was slowly organising itself into a Hurricane MU. While there I had my introduction to the Wimpy — as a security guard preventing the local populace from helping themselves to souvenirs from a pranged Wellington. I don't recall the cause of the crash — only that it was in the middle of nowhere, on a wet day, wetter evening to follow, and little protection from the elements all night except inadequate shelter from a leaky tarpaulin rigged up against a hedge, and mud, mud, mud everywhere. The following day was dry and we could then assess this strange aircraft in a more benevolent frame of mind; a frontline bomber, full of forbidden and secret things to our untutored eyes. It had belly-landed and the crew had escaped via the astrodome and cockpit roof hatch, and I had to climb over the wing, drop into the fuselage, replace the astro hatch and exit through the cockpit roof. Later, when Henlow sent out an armourer to remove the guns and ammo etc, I had to assist again and learned a little more about Barnes Wallis's brainchild; especially the contortionist method of entering the rear gun turret.

Below: Refuelling Wimpy R1598, KX-C of 311 (Czech) Sqn at East Wretham. *B. Rijnhout*

'When business at Henlow slackened I was promoted from LAC to Corporal and posted to 57 Squadron — "somewhere in England". My movement order specified a particular RAF station, so I dutifully toted all my kit and caboodle there — only to be informed 57 had moved elsewhere! This process was repeated on two more stations, and I finally caught up with the squadron at Feltwell — only to be asked by the Orderly Room where the hell I'd been! No 57 Squadron had only recently converted from Blenheims to Wimpys when I joined them, and were sharing Feltwell with No 75 (NZ) Squadron. Life here was fairly typical of any bomber station then. On duty it was a case of work, work and work, while off-duty hours meant the Corporal's Club or down to the village for a pint, a game of darts, and — if lucky — a visit to the "Caff", a private house with two front rooms converted to a restaurant were we could sample standard fare of double-egg and chips — a scarcity in those days of rations for all.

'In 1940 the country as a whole was only just beginning to realise that it really had a war on its plate, and the authorities were still working to peacetime scales of issue for equipment and clothing; the £5 toolkit comprising King Dick adjustable, pliers, an 8-inch screwdriver, worn-out double-ended O/J spanners, and a 16-ounce "Brummagem Screwdriver" (hammer . . .) to service aircraft vastly more complicated than peacetime Harts, Demons, Audax, etc. Wet weather clothing was virtually unheard of, few "ferking jerkins", gumboots were scarcer than hen's teeth, and even a change of blue overalls was hard to come by. Yet the troops (a generic term for airmen beloved of officers but deeply resented by Erks . . .) seemed to accept it all, taking such things in their stride and almost happy to be roughing it in the circumstances. Two aspects of Halton character-training never mentioned on the official syllabi — ie self-reliance and ingenuity — came to the fore under such conditions. It was no problem to splice-up a new towing bridle when Stores had none in stock, or file up a spanner to fit any awkwardly-placed nut — it was a perfectly normal, accepted approach to the job in those days.

'No 57 was gradually working up to full operational standard, and, though a few night ops were carried out, most of the bombing effort was done by 75 Squadron at that time, some crews of which took perverse delight in heralding their return — until stopped by the CO — by turning on the air-driven siren as they joined the circuit; talk about noisy neighbours! Another nuisance occurred one lunchtime when a Junkers Ju88 appeared and proceeded to bomb us. Chaos reigned supreme, windows shattered, but no other damage in our hangar; though a Wimpy in the civvy contractors' hangar, sporting newly repaired and re-covered mainplanes needed further repairs after the raid. Not content, the Ju88 made a second circuit at even lower level to give his gunner a crack, just as our duty crew was emerging from the hangar heading for the shelter. I bit the dust smartish (or rather, snow) under the nearest cover, and though I saw snow flicking nearby where bullets struck, his aim was slightly off — fortunately, because as I discovered afterwards my improvised cover was a 500-gallon petrol bowser!

'One merry morning I was calmly notified by the Orderly Room that I was posted to Persia! This turned out to be Pershore on the movement order, an equally mysterious place, because no one could tell me anything about it other than it was in Worcestershire. After a cross-country rail safari, changing from train to train to train, I eventually arrived to find that the camp was still very much under construction, and mud everywhere. Such was Records Office organisation that there were no aircraft to service for over three weeks, until concrete runways had been completed. Then we had a comedy of errors farce to remind us that the war was still on. The station was far from completed — just runways laid but no perimeter track, and few dispersal pans or roads — so "They" sent us a couple of Wimpys to be getting on with. The 'drome was still a sea of mud, and there was no place to park them other than on one of the runways not in use. That night was a fine one, with nearly a full moon, and Jerry decided to have a go at the Midlands. I can imagine that from 15,000ft or so those triangulated runways, virgin uncamouflaged concrete, must have stood out like neon signs in the moonlight. Some lynx-eyed Jerry evidently thought so and accordingly at about 2-3am carefully, nay leisurely, circled two or three times and then planted a trio of bombs. A petrol bowser went up in flames, and the kites became Cat 3 with splinter damage — it was helluva way to start an OCU.

'As the OCU empire grew bigger, the satellite 'drome at Defford was opened, and again I was selected as a pioneer; making do and mending for a couple of months before "civilisation" in the form of SHQ was established. We commuted daily from Pershore by 3-ton truck or the clapped-out Mk I "Annie" — which was a damned sight noisier and almost as bumpy as the consumptive truck; then hutted accommodation became available. No particular Wimpy incidents there come to mind; just the inevitable burst tyres in heavy landings or brake failures, and the odd forced landings in impossibly small local fields etc. From Pershore/Defford I moved yet again, this time to Chipping Warden near Banbury, where another Wimpy OCU was formed. By the time I arrived there it was a going concern, and most erks were Wimpy-experienced.

'Life at "Chippy" was perhaps mundane, but had its moments. Jobs were tackled out on dispersal which in later years would be hangar work only; wing off, fuel tank out, self-sealing replaced after patch repairs. One item of human interest comes to mind. There was a blonde nymphomaniac WAAF on the Flight-line, whose world revolved around her crotch. It was tempting fate to send her on a DI (Daily Inspection) of a kite if airmen were also working on it, and you wanted the Form 700 signed up in a hurry. In an attempt to shame, or at least embarrass her, we constructed an extra large facsimile of the male organ from remnants of self-sealing outer

Top: Carrying a spare 12-volt battery into a 142 Sqn Wimpy at Binbrook, December 1940. *via R. Bonser*

Above: Air and ground crew of a 412 Sqn Wellington, January 1943. Air crew members were Alan Gill (second from left), 'Mo' Moore (3rd from left), Phil Bond (3rd from right), Jock Sloan (2nd from right), and Norman L. Child (far right). *N. L. Child*

Right: Snow-clearance, a monotonous and regular morning chore in winter. Here erks of 142 Sqn at Binbrook, December 1940, cleaning 'D-Dog's' wings. *via R. Bonser*

Left: Hoisting a 1,000lb MC bomb into a Wimpy's belly, by means of the hand-crank winch at right

Below: Fixing the hoist hook to a 250lb GP bomb

Right: Kiwi. T2835, 'C-Charlie' of 75(NZ) Sqn, ready to go.

cover rubber sheet, a ball of Bostik properly "cured", cord and realistic paint finish. The work of art was carefully parcelled, stamped, and addressed to her, and artfully delivered with the rest of the day's mail to the Chiefy's office, who innocently handed it to her in the Flight stores — a daily routine then — in front of a crowd of erks already in the know. She opened it — and was delighted! "Just what we need in the billet" ...

'There were too several tragic incidents. One Wimpy which was bogged down on damp grass couldn't be budged by the Fordson tractor alone, so the cry "Two-Six" went out and all spare bods lent a hand. One new member of the Flight, straight out of training school, was pushing on the tailplane along with others, and as the Wimpy began to shift this kid had his titfer (hat) knocked off by the IFF aerial wire strung from fuselage to tailplane-tip. He bent down, picked it up, fumbled, then straightened up as the rear cone of the nacelle hit him. He fell and the starboard mainwheel went right over him — ever seen an imprint of a human head in soft earth? Not a pretty sight ... "Chippy" seemed to have more aircraft crashes than either Pershore or Defford. A pupil crew on a "loaded cross-country" exercise swung on take-off and finished up a blazing wreck against the ATC (Air

94

Traffic Control) building, trapping two fire-engines in the adjacent fire-house The "bomb load" was dummy — but it didn't do the crew a lot of good. Another prang — inexplicably with a staff crew of seasoned Bomber Command veterans sprinkled with DFCs, DFMs, etc — occurred when a railway marshalling yard was mistaken for the flarepath; or so the Chief Instructor decided.

'There were also occasions when Wimpys returned worse for wear after pupils had been "blooded" on short-range ops against coastal targets; shot-up controls, no hydraulics, or "continental" timber jammed through the nose just below the front gun position (I never could tell the difference between English and French oak or beech . . . !) One crew discovered it impossible to break the glass contents sight of the header tank with the escape axe, so punctured the metal tank itself to pour in coffee/tea/urine — only to find that the hydraulic loss wasn't a lack of fluid, just a duff EDP (engine-driven pump).

'Good relations with some of the staff crews meant a few opportunities at slack moments to get a few flying hours in, even as a second dickey in the dual-control Wimpys if on airtest for other reasons. And, of course, when "Butch" Harris was scraping the barrel for his "Thousand-bomber raids", "Chippy" was well and truly involved, and there was an air of increased excitement and dedication all round, even though the OCU Wimpys only went along to make up the numbers. Then, in 1944, I was on the move yet again, this time to SEAC (South-East Asia Command) and Wimpys passed out of my life.'

W. E. Wilkinson was an LAC (Leading Aircraftman) fitter when he first worked on Wellingtons with 142 Squadron at Binbrook in 1940:

'The squadron was equipped with Wellington Mk IIs with Rolls-Royce Merlin engines fitted with DH hydromatic airscrews, and during the working-up period — the unit began converting from Fairey Battles to Wimpy IIs in November 1940 — I became a fitter for Wimpy W5359, QT-B, of A Flight. By the time we were declared operational I'd been promoted to Corporal and was NCO in charge of three aircraft on one dispersal, including W5359.

'Possibly the biggest snag with the Mk II was its tendency to drop its nose in a dive, caused by the thrust-line of the Merlin being higher and the airscrew being further forward of the CG than on the Pegasus and Mercury engines of the Mk 1s. This meant a pilot had to trim the elevator back to fly straight and level. Unfortunately, the trim tabs were interconnected with the flaps in such a way that when flaps were lowered the elevators were also lowered to keep the aircraft on an even keel. No harm was done until the flaps were fully lowered after touch-down. If the pilot hadn't centralised the trim tabs before using the flaps he had quite an appreciable amount of trim on, so that when the flaps were fully lowered the hydraulic pressure of the flaps ripped the whole trimming box off the fuselage; even experienced crews were guilty of this, especially after a long op.

'Anybody who ever worked with Merlin engines will remember how easily they started, and the Mk II was, in my opinion, the easiest-started Wellington of them all; indeed, I think

Above: Z1091, 'A-Apple' of
419 ('Moose') Sqn, RCAF gets
an early morning DI (Daily
Inspection), 1942.
Public Archives of Canada

it was the only one which could be
started by just one man. During 1941,
however, we were re-equipped with
Mk IVs with Pratt & Whitney Twin
Wasp engines, and after our easy life
with Merlins we were rudely
awakened with the Wasps. The first
snag encountered was a tendency for
the bottom cylinders to fill with oil. We
had to hand-turn the propeller four
complete revolutions before attempting
to start, to be sure we had not got an
hydraulic lock in the cylinders. All too
often we had, which meant removing
cowlings and plugs to drain the bottom
cylinders and then changing the plugs.
Once this was accomplished, starting
was not too bad until damp and cold
weather started. As the Twin Wasp
had petrol injection, we needed a crew
member on the wobble pump to give us
petrol pressure. As soon as the engine
fired on engagement of the starter, the
mixture control was moved from cut-
out to auto-rich. This caused a jet of
petrol at 5lb/sq in to be injected into the
centre of the supercharger. However, if
the engine didn't catch first time, it
became so hopelessly flooded that
there was no hope of starting.

'This bad starting business was such
a problem that both Nos 12 and 142
Squadrons were equipped with special
Commer vans. These had a large petrol
blowpipe in the van which led, via
flame traps, to four large-diameter
flexible pipes. These pipes were
wrapped around the engine and the
blowpipe lit. Once it had been warmed
up to normal running temperature, it
would start up. By the time 142 was
equipped with Mk IV Wimpys it had
moved to Waltham, leaving 12
Squadron at Binbrook; Waltham being
Binbrook's satellite, just outside
Grimsby. One very bad mistake made
with the Mk IVs was to underestimate
their fuel consumption; so badly that
on the first IV operations Nos 12 and
142 Squadrons had only 25% of their
Wimpys get back to Binbrook. Several
landed in the North Sea, some at North
Coates. Flight Lieutenant Campling
belly-landed at North Coates, having
run out of petrol before he could get the
undercart down. One landed on
married quarters at Binbrook, while
two others landed at Binbrook with
dead engines. Where Merlins had con-
sumed about 85 gallons per hour, the
Twin Wasps were gulping down some
145 gallons per hour.

'Two other big snags we experienced with Twin Wasps were sludge in
the oil preventing the two-stage
supercharger changing speed, and the
secondary windings in the magnetos
breaking at the soldered joint due to
the soldering flux not being removed
during manufacture. Despite all my
foregoing apparent "prejudice" against
the Wasp, I would like to emphasise

that the Twin Wasp was in fact a very good engine, but it was certainly not designed to operate in English winter conditions.

'Incidents in the squadron life included several distinctly hairy occasions. When the *Scharnhorst* and *Gneisenau* were running from Brest, one of our Flight commanders flew directly over the *Scharnhorst* and jettisoned his complete bomb load. The Wimpy got badly shot up, but he couldn't believe that he hadn't caused a lot of damage. The bomb-aimer had sworn he had jettisoned, but unfortunately the pilot had not opened the bomb doors, so the master switch was "off" and they brought all the bombs back. Then we had one squadron commander, Wing Commander Gibson (not Guy Gibson, VC of 617 fame) who returned one night with damaged hydraulics. He managed to get the undercarriage down but not the flaps, and made a very hairy flapless landing in the dark. Next day he told his aircrews to practise flapless landings in daylight, just in case they met a similar situation. I was helping out on an engine at dispersal that day and, on looking up, saw a Wimpy charging down the runway at about 60kts, and already three-quarters of the runway behind him. I remarked to the fitter that if he doesn't lift off soon he won't make it. The fitter answered

"He isn't going up, he's coming down", which indeed he did — straight over the road and into a ploughed field! Then there was the new fitter who snatched a quick nap on the bunk of Wimpy "Q" instead of "O" — and went to Hamburg in just his overalls, instead of the expected circuit and bumps around Waltham . . .'

Reg Humphries completed his trade training as an electrician (Group I tradesman) at Credenhill in 1941, and on passing out was posted to Holme upon Spalding Moor:
'On arrival at Holme I found the construction workers still putting the finishing touches to the 'drome; one hangar being still without a concrete floor. We were to be part of an Australian squadron on its way to England, No 458, which finally arrived in August 1941 and eventually commenced ops in late October. The Wellington IVs we were to use had been arriving in ones and two, all brand new, all fitted with Pratt & Whitney Twin Wasp engines.

'As an electrician I was one of the section of eight to ten men. We had a flight sergeant, a prewar airman recalled for war service, one Corporal, and the rest of us AC1s or AC2s. As a Group 1 tradesman I found myself in charge of B Flight's aircraft, as well as the regular servicing inspections in the

Above: One for the squadron album — the ground crews of 38 Sqn in 1942. *L. Jordan*

hangars. Our day was usually the same routine throughout the week. Mornings would be taken up with repairs and servicing inside the hangars, carrying out normal 40-hours', 80-hours' and 120-hours' inspections, keeping an eye on the battery charging rooms; though these latter were later manned (if that's the right word . . . !) by WAAFs with a separate trade of Battery Charger, thus relieving us of this duty. As soon as operations were known, the kites had to be given DIs, which meant a trip to each aircraft in turn to check all electrics were functioning correctly. The Wimpy had a distinct wiring system known as "loom" wiring which was quite advanced in those days. It enabled sections of wiring to be changed without stripping the whole system.

'It was a 24-volts' powered system and amongst the items which had to be checked were navigation, formation, landing, interior and call lights. Undercarriage indicators and bombing gear were also checked for correct operation, propeller feathering motors, gun turrets and bomb sights, even the pitot head was included. The ground crew needed to run the starboard engine so we could check that the generator was

charging correctly, and another essential item included in our inspection was the trolley accumulator and its portable batteries, used for starting the engines. If all was well on the first aircraft, it was on to the next and right through the procedure again. Any necessary repairs were done as soon as possible — if not before!

'Once all aircraft had been checked out and declared serviceable, the night-flying equipment had to be checked. First, the "Glim Lamps", small lights placed alongside each side of the runway, powered by a two-volts' wet battery with a six-watt bulb fitted under a reflector so that they could only be seen from the sides. These were backed up by the forerunner of FIDO — Goose-necked flares, or "Duck Lamps" as they were often called. These were similar to metal watering cans, filled with paraffin with a piece of cloth pushed down the single spout, and were lit when it was misty to help get returning aircraft into the aerodrome. The other flare path equipment was the Chance Light — switched on to illuminate landing areas and switched off immediately the kite landed — and the "Angle of Glide Indicator"; a small illuminated coloured glass panel which showed red for "Too low", amber for "Too high", and green for "OK". A field telephone had to be laid from the control tower to the controller's cabin at the end of the runway in use, but often the wind changed just as one had tested the line and we'd have to set it all up again on runway Two. As well as equipment on the 'drome, we also had to check the marker beacon, a neon-tubed tower, moved every night, which flashed the code letters of the airfield.'

Selwyn Barrett joined No 37 Squadron at Feltwell in October 1940, when the unit was equipped with Wellington Ics, and remained with the squadron until October 1942:

'The squadron did not stay much longer at Feltwell, moving lock stock and barrel to Egypt a month after I arrived. The journey out there was not without incident. The sea party, travelling through the Mediterranean aboard HMS *Manchester*, joined in a naval battle off Cape Spartivento! The *Manchester* was slightly damaged but several Italian ships were even more so, and we eventually reached Egypt and rejoined our air party (who had flown out via Malta) at Fayid in the Suez Canal zone. A couple of weeks later, along with 38 Squadron, we moved further south to Shallufa, which was to be our main base for more than a year. Then, early in 1941, the main party of the squadron set off by road to Alexandria, then by boat in HMT *Dumana*, to go to Greece. We only made it as far as Crete and later had rather a hairy trip back to Shallufa — we didn't even see our Wellingtons for a couple of weeks!

'During the two years I spent with 37 in the Middle East we also — at various times — sent detachments to Malta and Iraq (this for the Raschid Ali business), but our main targets throughout this time were Benghazi and, later, Tobruk — the famous "Milk Runs". For these the normal drill, when bombing Benghazi for instance, was to make a refuelling stop at one of the advanced landing grounds (ALGs), usually LG 09, an airstrip about 20 miles inland from El Daba and the coast road. In January 1942, in fact, the two operational flights moved en bloc to LG 09, leaving the maintenance flight, etc back at Shallufa. From 09 we operated successfully until the retreat back to El Alamein in June 1942.

'To alleviate the strain of operating from a desert strip, where water was always short, beer not exactly plentiful, and the food pretty awful, crews were given five days leave in Tel Aviv occasionally. These were most enjoyable breaks with the added bonus of a few bags of oranges for the messes. To enable people to wash off the layer of sand which built up whilst at LG 09, a truck would take parties to the beach a couple of times a week when everything for the night's work was ready. The journey was terrible — over 20 miles of rough desert track when one didn't know whether to stand or sit; the bouncing was equally bad and painful. Swimming in the sea was a joy, and salt-water soap produced a reasonable lather to clean off the layers of sand. Ten minutes after start-

Below: 'Dress will be informal' — the armourers of 38 Sqn, Libya, 1942. *L. Jordan*

Bottom: Repair gang at No 5 METS, Shallufa with a Wellington which had been shot down by a German nightfighter. They had it back on ops within a week . . .

Right: Sand-boys. Erks of 70 Sqn at LG 237.   *G. F. Wilson*

Below: Scruffs! 70 Sqn erks in Libya, 1941.   *G. F. Wilson*

ing back, however, we'd have a fresh fine coating of sand, and by the time we reached the ALG all we were fit for was sleep.

'Being away from civilisation we were a bit out of touch with news, and it was the travelling padre who told us that Tobruk had fallen — which we found hard to believe, and it was only his dog collar which convinced us that it wasn't enemy propaganda! There followed hectic days and nights, and second sorties were flown from an even remoter ALG, from where when I left on the last Wimpy the corporal in charge with one assistant were about to destroy hundreds of 50-gallon barrels of fuel then drive east themselves. Landing back at 09 that morning we found everything packed and ready for moving out. Some of our ground transport had already left, and army units were streaming down the edge of the landing strip as the Wimpys were overloaded for the flight back to the Canal zone. After a couple of nights and operations from what is now Cairo airport, the squadron moved to Abu Sueir and operated regularly from there until the Allied advance in October 1942.

'The joy of Abu Sueir was running water, having spent six months out "in the blue" on a water-bottle full per day! Once we were organised the squadron operated smoothly again. It was during this period that the Wimpy was used in a tactical role against the Afrika Korps, with Fleet Air Arm Albacores dropping flares, and Wimpys dropping anti-personnel bombs and strafing enemy positions. The anti-personnel bombs used were either canisters of 40lb bombs or 250lb GPs with an 18-inch mushroom rod screwed into noses. The 40-pounders cost us several lives and a couple of aircraft in bombing-up accidents, falling to the ground while being fitted into canisters.

'Tobruk became the "Mail Run" and the AA defences were said to be the heaviest in the Middle East. Navigation aids were few and far between, but the stars were often bright and QDRs were obtainable on the way home. Low stratus over the Delta sometimes created problems; one of our Wimpys crashed into a plateau at the top of the Attaqa mountains early one morning, when letting down, killing the second pilot who was lying in the bomb-aimer's position looking for pinpoints. Other unforgettable incidents include the night one Wimpy taxied across the runway as another was taking off; both were fully bombed up. Then the evening that a visiting Boston crashed into the second of a line of ten Wimpys which were all fuelled and bombed-up ready for take-off. Four Wimpys were written off, two more badly damaged, and it might have been worse had not Flight Sergeant Robinson, B Flight SNCO, started and taxied away one which was already burning, thus enabling the fire tenders to get in close.'

G. F. Wilson was an LAC serving in the Sudan with No 223 Squadron (Vickers Wellesleys) in late 1940, when he was posted to Egypt and Wellingtons:
'In November 1940 I was posted from 223 to 70 Squadron at Kabrit, Egypt, in the Suez Canal zone, and two months later went to Greece with a squadron detachment to an airfield not far from Athens. For some months we waited while the Greek authorities tried to make up their minds whether or not the Wimpys should be allowed to bomb the Italians — they never did — and while the aircraft were idle the ground crews improved their expertise in crawling under the coils of barbed wire round the perimeter every time enemy fighters were spotted over Athens! Sometime in April 1941 the aircraft returned to Egypt, while the ground crews were flown back in a Sunderland; a trip enlivened by one of the air gunners telling us that Ju88s were active in the area, and that our hope of survival in the event of an attack was to open the portholes and blaze away with our rifles!

'We arrived safely at Kabrit and I was posted to 148 Squadron on the same station, remaining with 148 from April 1941 until re-posted to Malta HQ in December 1942. We were quite busy during 1941-42, spending much of our time on various desert landing grounds. On one occasion, travelling into the desert, we passed our army going in the opposite direction. My first taste (literally . . .) of desert existence came when we were miles off the desert track, in a marquee erected by the advance party where we ate. For dinner we had what was to become staple desert fare — meat and vegetables, followed by rice pudding. I asked another erk sitting opposite to me why he was picking currants out of his rice and putting them on the side of

Below: Just another job for the metal-bashers . . . a Wimpy which got back from Benghazi — just.

Top: Major inspection and repair job at Aqir, 1943.

Above: Bones. Scrapheap of busted Wimpys — a treasure trove of much-needed spares for the erks.

his plate. When he told me that they were flies, I felt distinctly queasy, having almost finished my rice, flies and all . . .

'There was always a scarcity of water at ALGs. Each tent held eight men, and occasionally a lorry would bring water in 50-gallon drums that had once contained oil. Each tent received five gallons of oily water, in which we were supposed to wash; needless to say there wasn't a lot of washing among the erks. Each day we received one pint of drinking water, and considerable self-control was

needed to make it last until the next day's ration. I used to shampoo my hair in paraffin, and my clothes in petrol — the latter being a sure way of keeping free of body lice.'

Jim 'Curly' Gardner was a prewar regular armourer stationed at Abu Sueir when the war came to the Middle East. He remained in North Africa, Egypt, Libya, et al until the end of the North African campaigns before finally returning to the UK. Serving with a variety of units during his four years' sojourn in the sun, his memories of his

'Butlin's Tour' (his expression) are probably similar in character to a majority of erks in that theatre:

'Whatever the snags and uncivilised conditions of service in the Middle East, these were mainly outweighed in my mind by the climate — hot days, cool nights, and the knowledge that the sun would always rise tomorrow — and, especially, the terrific camaraderie of all ranks; at least, when we were at the operational sharp end. If you were with a firstline squadron, life revolved around the kites and the job you were all there to do. Parades, bullshit, proper uniform, proper channels, etc were for the gabardine-clothed penguins back in Cairo — out in the bundoo such items were disregarded. Cairo and Alex (*Alexandria*) were OK for a spot of leave, IF you could get leave, but even there any ranker was looked upon as a second-class citizen; it was a case of "officers only" in most decent hotels or restaurants, hence I often promoted myself by slipping Flight Lieutenant's double-rings on my shirt epaulettes when in town — nobody bothered you if you were wearing zobbitt's rank. I was only rumbled once, when one of our Flight commanders came into the same bar I was in — another officers-only joint — and sat on the stool next to me. His reaction was simply, "What are you having, Curly?" — and bought me a Stella! (He was killed over Tobruk three weeks later — an ex-Cranwell gentleman in every sense of that word.)

'Life on a forward airstrip was simply summed up — work. Everything boiled down to one priority, to keep the aircraft flying, no matter what it took. We were always suffering shortages — food, water, spares, etc — but improvisation was the order of the day. Though every tradesman had his distinct responsibilities, there were no demarcation lines on jobs — when it came to bombing up a line of Wimpys, for example, everyone pitched in; cooks, clerks and air crews if necessary. Accommodation was equally simple — a spade to dig a square hole in the desert, two planks of wood covered in a sack for your bed, and a pup tent rigged over the hole for a home; tents being varied in size and state of repair according to availability. On some occasions even these luxuries were absent, and sleeping was a question of making a hole comfortable enough to accommodate your hip bone. Food was monotonous,

yet apparently adequate, because I cannot remember ever being really hungry — only perpetually thirsty.

'Working dress on a forward airstrip was a joke. The variety of styles — worn by officers or erks — resembled a circus parade; ranging from issue KD (khaki drill) to lovingly-knitted weird pullovers and jackets provided by relatives in the UK or some comforts-for-the-troops fund or organisation. Basically, everything was some shade of brown — RAF blue uniform was a rarity, usually worn only by new-comers to the unit. A pair of faded

Above: Jim Currie (left) and Don Cox, the ground crew of *'Flak-Happy Harry'* of 104 Sqn, Foggia, Italy, February 1945. *S. J. Sterrett*

103

Above: 'Where's that bloody nut?' . . . engine fitter attempting to service a Wimpy's Pegasus XVIII. *IWM*

shorts, stockings and boots/shoes were normal and sufficient dress during the day, but at night it could often get cold enough to necessitate some form of greatcoat or fur-lined jacket. The sun faded everything to a neutral sand-colour, even issue black boots after a while!

'Long service in the desert inevitably produced some right characters — eccentric would be too mild a word for a few of the sand-happy blokes I met here and there. One corporal engine-fitter we had kept a trained scorpion, taking it for early morning walks on the end of a long piece of string; while one of the Wimpy air crew — a navigator from a very snooty country-gent background — used to try rounding up his private pack of pi-dogs for hunting . . . One lad returned from some leave in Cairo with a pet chameleon permanently tethered by a bootlace to his bush-jacket lapel, where it continually crawled around his neck and shoulders picking off flies with deadly accuracy with its long

tongue. Women, of course, were just never seen at the operational front, yet I cannot recall *any* cases of homo-sexuality among the blokes; though the immediate postwar population explo-sion back in the UK was hardly surpris-ing!

'For all its apparent deprivations of body and soul, my time in the desert with the squadrons was a very happy period of my life. I met many men who showed the very best aspects of human nature (though I also met a few who demonstrated the worst sides too), but my chief memory, which even today saddens me, is of those young Wimpy air crews who went missing. Many of them were literally kids straight out of school, yet they were always cheerful, and accepted the odds against survival calmly each time they took took off. Looking at the state of Britain today, especially some of the antics of modern youth, I tend to get very bitter about the loss of those lads who gave their all for, apparently, no good purpose now.'

Tales from the Crews

Wing Commander K. H. Wallis, C Eng, FRAeS, FRSA, RAF Retd, today is internationally known, particularly for his '007'-type gyrocopter inventions, but in 1941 he was plain Pilot Officer Ken Wallis, a Wellington skipper serving with No 103 Squadron, based at Elsham Wolds, Lincolnshire. On the night of 20/21 September 1941, Ken set out in Wimpy L7886 'X' to bomb Frankfurt, but the primary target was obscured by cloud so he carried his bomb load back to the coast and released it over a secondary objective. On return to Britain the whole of southern England was covered in fog, and the added journey to his secondary target had used up precious fuel, leaving Ken with no margin to fly further north for a fog-free airfield to land on.

Using his 'Darkie' emergency radio system, he received a response from Binbrook, after following the searchlight homing set-up. These searchlights could be seen under the fog layers, and by then there was no fuel registering on Wallis's fuel gauges, though the instruments *might* have been inaccurate. Over Binbrook he requested the Chance Light to be switched on and off, noted its position, then made ten attempts to land, using timed circuits. Obviously there were many hazards to such a landing, and eventually he called up Binbrook tower requesting permission to bale out his crew before he made any further attempt at landing. Binbrook's reply was to tell him to fly to Linton-on-Ouse. Wallis pointed out that he had no fuel indicated, repeating what he'd already told the tower when he had first arrived over Binbrook.

While this unproductive conversation was going on the Wellington was steadily climbing; then, suddenly, both engines cut, came on again briefly, though screaming in fine pitch. Wallis's decision had been made for him — he told Binbrook they were

baling out. The crew started to leave, while Ken started to don his parachute; a harness/life jacket combined type, with hooks on the hips for the seat-type 'chute. The release handle from the 'chute had to be fastened by turn-buttons on the harness when required, and was usually stuffed between the 'chute and its attached cushion when not in use. Ken fastened his main 'chute hooks but was unable to extract the release handle from under the cushion. As he lifted up in his seat the parachute and cushion came up too. He therefore had to undo the main hooks, extract and fix the release, then refix the main hooks.

While all this was going on the Wellington was gliding down, with occasional tiny boost from bursts of power on the last fuel dregs. Ken left it to its own devices rather than switching off — every foot of height was crucial. When he was finally ready to leave he looked back down the cathedral-like fuselage, in which one thoughtful crew member had left an interior light on — it was empty. Ken could now leave. The altimeter read 700ft. Lifting himself down from his high, left-hand seat, he opened the front hatch, but felt unusually encumbered, even though wearing his 'chute. Looking back he saw in the faint light that his pack was still on his vacated seat, and he was firmly connected to it by yards of webbing all tangled with the seat-raising handle. If he'd jumped immediately he would have trailed under his crashing Wimpy. Gathering all the lines he could reach, Ken knelt on the lip of the hatch and let himself topple forward.

Once out Ken let go his collection of 'chute webs and pulled his rip cord. The parachute opened with a painful jerk, and at that moment the doomed Wellington passed close overhead. Ken's immediate relief at getting clear was as quickly damped by the sounds of his Wellington approaching him. It

Above left: The remains of Ken Wallis's Wellington, L7886, at Holton-Le-Moor on 21 September 1941. *via S. Finn*

Left: Sqn Ldr Jones and Sgt Dichiel of 99 Sqn at Digri (?), India in 1942. *IWM*

Above: Wellington R1013 of 40 Sqn, shot down on the night of 13 March 1941, after Sqn Ldr Hugh Lynch-Blosse and his crew had baled out. *Grp Capt H. Lynch-Blosse*

had circled and now came out of the fog, flying directly towards him — his senses were extended to the size of his parachute. The aircraft was slightly banked and as it continued its circle it narrowly missed him, then tore itself to pieces on the ground. For a moment there was a blessed silence, then Ken felt a hard blow as the unseen ground came up and hit him. He suffered concussion and some spinal injury. After being out for about half an hour he regained his senses, noticing fog dripping off a nearby hedge. Realising that he had no idea which way to go, he remembered his World War 1 Mauser pistol which he carried inside his flying suit. He fired two shots into the air, someone shouted in the distance, and he was soon discovered by a Home Guard and a local policeman. The rest of the crew had landed along the Caistor-Market Rasen road, all uninjured — the first 103 Squadron crew to bale out over Britain. Pilot Officer Ken Wallis was back on the operations list on 10 October.

Les Read was a Warrant Officer air gunner who completed a full tour of operations with 142 Squadron from Binbrook in 1941, though his ultimate survival was much in question on several of those sorties:

'On one raid over Cologne we were caught in a cone of searchlights at 14,000ft. The city below us was ablaze, and the absence of flak in our

area indicated that there were German fighters about. For what seemed hours, we dived, twisted, turned, climbed; all the while expecting to be raked with fighter cannons. Eventually our skipper, Flt Lt Dodson, yelled in frustration to our navigator, "You got me into this, now bloody well get me out!" After what must only have been about four to five minutes we dived away from the cone into the relative safety of darkness. As we came out of the limelight I saw an Me109 coming up from beneath us on the starboard side. I fired a long burst, saw the 109 shudder and then slip away to the side. I've always believed I hit him, though I couldn't claim it as a cert.

'Another particularly hairy trip was when we were briefed to bomb Wilhelmshaven. The Met boys told us weather would be favourable, but as we crossed over the island of Texel we realised visibility was going to be very bad. We were flying at 12,000ft and were met by a barrage of AA fire, and our port engine was hit. It became obvious after several attempts to restart it that it was u/s (unserviceable) and we began losing height. There was no option but to return to base so we turned. As we recrossed the North Sea visibility had been reduced to nil and it seemed highly unlikely we were going to make it on one engine. The only hope was to jettison everything loose, including our bombs. The lot went overboard, even my two heavy tanks of ammunition. By then the altimeter was reading zero, but we couldn't see any water and fully expected to crash any second. By some miracle we neared our coastline, switched on the IFF and waited. There was a sudden frantic yell from the front gunner, Holgate, and we banked swiftly to the right — narrowly missing a barrage balloon! We were over Grimsby. We made it back to base at rooftop level.

'One of our daylight raids over France was a very near thing — I still don't know how we managed to get through. The Channel was a hot-bed of dogfights and planes were going down all over the place. We were hit and had to crash-land at St Eval; where I saw another Wimpy, badly shot up. Its rear gunner had his head completely shot off, and in the turret shambles was a half-eaten orange, covered in blood. All in all, I feel we, as a crew, were lucky to come through our tour scathed. We then split up and I was sent to Yate, Bristol, at the Parnall factory for a pre-instructor's course on Boulton Paul turrets; then posted to 25 OTU, Finningley as a gunnery instructor in early 1942.

'I decided to live out with my wife here — until then I wouldn't chance it, having seen so many wives shattered by their husbands not returning — and thought that, being off ops, we could spend a few weeks together at long last. Then came the reckoning — the first 1,000-raid on Cologne. Training units were roped in to make up the magic number, and I was put into a crew with four ex-operational chaps and two pupils. I can recall the skipper's name, Pilot Officer Hughes, while the front gunner was a Sgt Greenhalgh — a pupil on his first op. We bombed Cologne and the city was alight from end to end — an awesome sight which I can never forget. On the return journey we were hit by flak over Holland, and after unsuccessful attempts to restart the shattered engine it caught fire, and in no time we were ablaze. It was about 2am with full moonlight, and we all baled out. As I neared the ground some ground gunners opened fire, but I landed unscathed in a factory in Eindhoven. The Dutch workers eagerly stripped me for souvenirs, then, as I was about to climb over the factory wall a German guard rushed up and I was clobbered. I was next taken to an underground ARP centre where I stayed until dawn, and where I was given a bottle of pilsner and a hunk of bread. Later I was taken to the Amsterdam gaol, where I was interrogated for six days in a hot unventilated cell, before being eventually transferred to Stalag Luft III — the start of three long years behind the wire.'

Eric Barclay was trained as a navigator, passing through ITW at Brighton via No 2 OAFU in Cumbria, to 21 OTU at Enstone (satelite to Moreton-in-the-Marsh) in May 1943. Here he received his first experience in Wellingtons — mainly old Mk 1cs — and crewed up:
'In July 1943 my crew were posted to No 310 FTU, Harwell, where we received, direct from Vickers, a brand-new Wellington X, HE947, on which we carried out a 16-hours' acceptance test before flying it to Hurn, prior to taking it out to India. The trip to India went by way of Hurn-Port Lyautey-Ras El Mar-Castel Benito-Tobruk-El Agheila-El Adem-Cairo-Ismailia-Lydda-Habbaniyah-Shaibah-Kuwait-Bharein-Sharjah-Jask Island-Karachi-Allahabad; though en route we changed aircraft to Wellington X, HE957. In October 1943 the crew arrived in Jessore, north of Calcutta, where Nos 99 and 215 Squadrons were then stationed, both operating Wimpy Xs, with 16 aircraft to each squadron.

'Both squadrons were flying operations against targets in Burma, from Mandalay to Rangoon, mostly against lines of communication but including various towns and centres. One aircraft on 215 was converted to take a 4,000lb cookie and was usually a lone raider. We were posted to this squadron. On one trip, on 24 December 1943, we loaded up for a trip to Mandalay and needed to clear at least 10,000ft if we were to get over the Arakan hills. One hour after take-off the starboard engine had to be feathered and, naturally, with a full load of bombs and petrol we lost some 8,000ft rapidly — we hadn't reached those hills yet. The pilot, Flight Sergeant Nixon, managed to get the aircraft under control after unloading all bombs safely and some petrol. However, he needed help to hold full opposite rudder and some rope was tied to the starboard rudder bar, and two of the crew literally leaned on it to maintain straight and level flight. We

Above: German newspaper photo of R1013's crew after capture. From left: Sgt Caldicott (F/AG), Sgt Hammond (W/Op), Flg Off Stan Palmer (R/AG), Sgt Clay (Obs) and Sqn Ldr Hugh Lynch-Blosse.
Grp Capt H. Lynch-Blosse

had no radio (which was charged from the starboard engine) but finally landed at Chittagong at first attempt.

'Chittagong at that time was being used by fighters, and on landing there a ground wallah came tearing out to us to order us off the runway in no uncertain terms. Apparently some fighters were due to land. After our dicey trip we were decidedly edgy, and this bristling twit was informed strongly that if he could taxi a twin-engined aircraft on one engine he had better come and .... well try it!

'The 14th Army then were surrounded by the Japanese inside the Imphal valley, where Hurricane-bombers were operating from Kangla, Palel and Imphal airstrips. No 215 Squadron was given the task of supplying them with the necessary 250lb HE bombs, and daily we ferried loads of these bombs to these airstrips inside the valley. Our crew flew a total of 25 such trips during May-June 1944, returning to our base each evening, taking with us up to two soldiers on leave to Calcutta. By the end of June 1944 I was tour-expired, and 215 had begun re-equipping with Liberators. As for the Wimpy, I considered it a good all-round aircraft, a veritable workhorse for the RAF at that time, and apart from the feathering incident always found it highly reliable.'

Denys White was a pilot with No 150 Squadron in Italy in 1944:
'When I arrived on 150 Squadron in April 1944 we operated from Ammendola airfield, with a runway of wire mesh. We used this strip in con-

junction with Fortresses and Lightnings of the American 15th Air Force; they bombed by day and we took the night shift. However, early in July 1944 Nos 142 and 150 Squadrons moved to Regina airfield north of Foggia and there we were on our own. Regina was just a dirt runway and caused many problems for our aircraft tyres; the stones, etc cutting the rubber. I always had to check the tyres prior to take-off of other aircraft whenever I wasn't flying ops — it was a dusty, filthy job but very necessary.

'Operating Wimpys in Italy in 1944 was something akin to Burma's "Forgotten Army". We had no navigational aids at all, and incendiaries were dropped to obtain our drifts over land, and flame floats etc by night. The most experienced crews usually got to the target area first and dropped flares, then we had to bomb visually by the light of the flares. It wasn't until about July 1944 that we received Gee and even then it was of limited range. A squadron of Halifaxes started to act as our pathfinders in late July, equipped with H2S, but their early efforts were a disastrous failure. We were supposed to drop our bombs on their target indicators (TIs), but these were usually miles from the target. Our crew became very demoralised until the Hallies finally began dropping their TIs properly on target.

'In addition to bombs we were expected to take along a load of propaganda leaflets — "Nickels" as they were termed. When dropping "Nickels" our instructions were to go upwind of the target area to release them. As can be imagined, having dropped our bombs no one wanted to hang about the target with mere leaflets. We devised a very good system to solve this nuisance. On dispersal prior to a sortie, we'd almost close the bomb doors after bombing up, then placed the packets of ''Nickels'' along the inside edge of the doors, opened the packets, then fully closed the bomb doors. Thus, over the target, we dropped the whole issue in one go. This system worked remarkably well until one night when the sortie was scrubbed at the last minute. Next morning the armourers had to change the bomb load, opened the bomb doors, and the leaflets scattered from Foggia to Naples . . . at least we weren't short of bog paper for the next few weeks!

'From a pilot's point of view, the Wimpy was a very strong aircraft and would take any amount of punishment from flak. However, it had its awkward characteristics too. On take-off one always had to throttle back sharply in order to work the accelerator pump, otherwise the engines were likely to cut out when opening up to full power. The Hercules engine was very good, though it suffered from trouble with the magneto occasionally. On landing one had to engage a sort of automatic trim, which meant one had to push hard on the control column during the approach run. Then, on levelling out, one took great care otherwise the nose came well up. The automatic pilot was also a dicey affair, sometimes causing the Wimpy to dive steeply. For such emergencies a fire axe was kept handy to sever the hydraulics pipeline if the automatic pilot couldn't be disengaged smartly. One other disquieting habit was for the escape hatch over the pilot to fly off on occasion.'

Hugh Lynch-Blosse joined the RAF as a Cranwell cadet, being trained at the College from 1935-37, and by early 1941 was a Squadron Leader and flight commander with No 40 Squadron, based at Alconbury:

Date	A/C Type	Pilot	Crew	Duty
12 March	Wellington R1013	Self	Heaton Palmer Clay Hammond Caldicott	Night bombing — Berlin

Left: Crew from 150 Sqn at Ammendola airfield, Foggia, Italy on 22 June 1944. From left: Flt Sgts D. Evans (W/Op) and G. Coleman (R/AG), Flg Off D. White (Capt), Ltd G. Hunt, SAAF (Nav), Flg Off P. Wheatley (B/Aimer). *D. White*

Below left: Marseilles under attack on 14/15 August 1944, viewed from 10,300ft by a 150 Sqn Wellington. *L. Hallam*

Above: 'Madame X', Wellington 'W' of 150 Sqn at St Valentin on 20 August 1944, about to fly this crew's last op. From left: Ives (R/AG), Hindle (Nav), Walker (Capt) L. Hallam (B/Aimer), Henderson (W/op). *L. Hallam*

Left: The briefing room for 104 Sqn at Foggia, Italy, 1944. *G. Pearson*

Right: Eric Tomlin and his 104 Sqn crew, Foggia. At far right, G. Pearson. *G. Pearson*

Above: Bivvy. Eric Tomlin (Capt), Geoff Garner (R/AG) and George Pearson (Wop/AG), 104 Sqn. *G. Pearson*

Above right: Rear gunner. 'Mac' and his turret of Wellington LP303, 'T' of 104 Sqn. *G. Pearson*

'So reads my log-book for that day in 1941, similar to a thousand other entries since the very first one at Cranwell in September 1935 — but with two differences. Bertie Bowler, my deputy in A Flight, has written "Aircraft failed to return", and there was no flight time recorded (actually four hours and 45 minutes). The reason was simple — we were shot down by flak in the early hours of 13 March — on my 13th operational sortie in a Wellington . . . in R10*13*!

'The target was Berlin and three aircraft of my flight were briefed for the trip, thereby fulfilling one of my two ambitions at that time — the other being to bomb Italy. We took off at about 2100hrs along the flare-path at Alconbury. As was usually the case, the hours between briefing and take-off were accompanied — in my case at least — by tension, anxiety and some fear. Once the throttles were opened, however, all that disappeared, and the constant thrill of flying, concentration, the togetherness of the crew, and our determination to achieve our object took over.

'It was a brilliant moonlight night and I clearly remember how surprised we were, cruising contentedly over Holland and Germany, not to be attacked by nightfighters. We could see Berlin from about 10-20 miles away and braced ourselves for the inevitable ordeal to come. Then, over the suburbs, a searchlight caught us and in spite of continuous weaving we couldn't escape — eventually I could count about 40 lights, with no one but us to find (or so it seemed . . .). Then the flak started and the noise, glare, smell and necessary weaving were the worst we'd yet experienced. Dusseldorf, Cologne, Brest and the rest seemed mild compared with this.

'I realised it must be very difficult for the navigator to chart his way to the target, yet in spite of the unholy racket all was calm inside the aircraft, which by now had been hit several times. After what seemed an age Clay identified the target and we started the run-up. By that time, because of our weaving, we were down to 7,000ft, and having to fly straight and level was neither easy or pleasant. Another age passed, then Clay finally said, "Bombs gone". We didn't wait to see results and I looked round for the best route to escape the flak and searchlights. Then, just as I thought we'd made it, an engine was hit, the prop stopped, and at the same time Henry Heaton announced — quite calmly I thought — "I've been hit". I had told him to stand between the engines as the safest place — yet he was our only casualty! Flak had also hit the front turret, exploding all its ammunition, but the gunner, Caldicott, was unharmed.

'As we left the area — now without opposition — I saw Tubby Wills from

Africa. Selected notes from his various experiences illustrate well some of the many hazards associated with 'Ops in a Wimpy':

'27 August 1942.
Aircraft Z1469, "A"
Target: Kassel (German Army HQ & garrison)
Bomb load: Mixed 500lb HE & incendiaries

'Airborne 2145. Routed in 10 miles south of Munster and same route out. Climbed to 9,000ft. Flak ships were active off Dutch coast. Vis good. Lot of flak ahead — somebody must have wandered off course over Munster. Good pinpoint. Approaching target and all hell let loose approx 10 miles ahead. Very heavy barrage, town ringed with guns and searchlights. Several kites have been hit and gone down. Running into target, terrific smell of cordite, searchlights are blinding, but drop bombs on schedule at 8,500ft. Weave out of target area and for a few minutes everything in chaos. Set course for home. Difficult to get a good pinpoint, and aircraft ahead running into heavy flak (shouldn't *be* any flak on this course!). Check wind again. There's been a sudden wind-change round to the North and whole force has been blown over Ruhr Valley. Search-lights and flak are forcing us lower and lower, and many aircraft are seen going down. Flak is so bad and search-lights so blinding that we decide to go right down full power to below 1,000ft. Front and rear turrets are firing at the searchlights and between them account for five. We burst our way out of the Ruhr, knowing we'd been hit many times, and climb to 8,000ft again. Make for Over Flakkee, then for base, but are forced to land at Harwell. Our aircraft looks a mess, full of holes and big chunks shot out, but except for cuts and abrasions none of crew is hurt. Next day flown back to base to discover, to our horror, that of the six aircraft of B Flight our crew are the only survivors. Duration of flight, six hours, 40 mins.

'8 September 1942
Aircraft "H"
Target: Frankfurt
Bomb load: One 4,000lb Cookie

'Airborne 2020. Set course for Over Flakkee and climbed to 10,000ft. Cloud thicker than expected over Holland

our squadron going in to the target at about 10,000ft and thought, ''Poor bugger, hope he makes it'' (he did). Some 50 miles from Berlin the good engine started to surge wildly and I now found it difficult — and later impossible — to maintain height. Soon we were down to 2,000ft and still descending and I realised we couldn't make it home, so I decided to bale out the crew. They went first, with instruc-tions to look after the wounded Henry — which led to them being captured almost at once. I stayed behind a little in order to lay about me with the axe in the cockpit, then jumped. The Welling-ton circled around me in a gentle glide, and I watched it crash in a field.

'I landed, buried my parachute in the approved manner, and headed westwards, listening with a mixture of envy, fear, relief (and, I suppose, some shock) to our aircraft returning home to bacon and eggs and beer and popsies — it was infuriating. Towards dawn I started to look for a place to hide, but had obviously left it too late because I was captured soon after it became light. I was first taken to the Luftwaffe base at Salzweden and after being pushed in the cooler fell asleep. When I woke the rest of the crew were there, except Henry who was in hospital. So began four years of *gefangenschaft . . .*'

Norman Child served with 142 Squadron, both in the UK and in North and we fly in cloud up to German border. Break in the cloud and we get good pinpoint on the Maas. Steered well clear of Cologne but plenty of flak to port suggests that a number of aircraft have wandered off course in cloud and are over city. Cloud now clearing, only 3/10ths cover. North of Mainz are attacked by nightfighter who score a hit on our tail fin. Rear gunner gives him a burst and we weave and dive our way to safety. Approaching target we detect a Halifax just overhead with its bomb doors open. Take quick avoiding action and prepare for our own run-in. Very heavy defences and well predicted flak. Enormous flash in sky and flaming debris falling — looks as though two aircraft have collided. Dropped our Cookie into middle of a huge circle of explosions and fires and dived away into the night. Checked damage on tail but, though it looked a ragged sight, was still functioning. Steered course for home north of Koblenz and south of Cologne. Brief encounter with flak ship off Dutch coast and a few more holes punched in us. None of crew hurt. Message from base; weather closed in, visibility very poor, divert to Waterbeach. Landed Waterbeach. Riggers inspected tail unit. Damage so severe they were amazed that the whole structure hadn't collapsed — the Wellington is a tough baby. Duration, six hours, 55mins.

'24 October 1942
Aircraft "L"
Target: Milan
Bomb load: Mixed, 500lb HE and canisters of incendiaries

'Airborne 1630. Landed Manston 1730 and took on fuel for overload tanks. Airborne again 1915 and climbed to 9,000ft over France. Clear starlit night. Fighter reported on starboard bow cruising at same speed, so we throttle back, descend 500ft and lose him. Halfway to target we start to climb to 15,500ft to clear Swiss Alps — extremely cold. Good pinpoint on Lake Geneva to port and mountain range looming ahead. Mont Blanc identified quite easily in clear night air, and set new course to target. Box barrage over target quietens down when bombing commences — unlike German targets — and we bomb through comparatively little opposition. Many fires started and large explosions seen. Bombed at 12,000ft. Turned on course for base and climbed back to 15,500ft. At course change at Haute Savoie we notice port engine is leaking oil badly and beginning to overheat. Port engine is throttled right back and we start very slow descent across France to keep up a reasonable airspeed. Everyone keyed up and anxious. We reach French coast at 3,000ft and pinpoint St Valery. Everything quiet, so we steal out to sea untouched. Port engine temperature is now so high we decide on a forced landing at West Malling. WM cleared us for emergency landing, and when we taxied to a halt the port engine died. Fitters found an oil feed line had been damaged by a shell splinter and engine was starved of oil. Across France we'd had a choice of feathering the prop and therefore probably a forced landing there, or pressing on, risking an engine fire. We had made the right choice — just. Duration, seven hours, 50mins

Below: Blida airfield, Algiers, 1944 — 'home' of Nos 142 and 150 Wellington squadrons with No 330 Wing in 1943. *W. Howarth*

'7 November 1942
Aircraft "L"
Target: Brest harbour approach (Mine-laying)
Briefing: Mines to be laid at entrance to Brest harbour, three miles south of Pt. de St Mathieu. Dropping height, 700ft with 10-seconds' intervals.

Airborne 2110. Climbed to 6,000ft and set course for Portland Bill. Cloud thickening inland but clearer over sea. Set course for Ushant Island from Portland Bill. Mid-way to Ushant radio receiver reported u/s but transmitter OK. Decided to continue to target whilst fault on receiver is traced. Ushant Island indentified approx five miles to port. Dark night but vis reasonably good. No joy with receiver. Wide turn out to sea and descend to dropping height. Engines throttled right back and mines dropped on DR time track to harbour approach. Open up engines and tight turn to port to avoid the town. Halfway on turn and climbing, a terrific explosion aft and aircraft almost out of control. Groundfire continues for a few minutes but we are not hit again. Set course for base and climb to 4,000ft at reduced revs. Damage is inspected and we find an enormous hole blasted out of the underbelly and side. Freezing gale is raging through the aircraft, and we bring the rear gunner forward of the damage. Over southern England weather has worsened, thick cloud and light rain. Descend to 2,000ft still in cloud. Call base, report damage and the u/s receiver. Checked under-carriage would lock down, then landed. Cloud ceiling at base 700ft with heavy rain. Duration, seven hours, 45mins. After-note: with our u/s receiver we didn't know that there'd been a general recall, so we were the only aircraft from No 1 Group flying that night. We should have aborted with a u/s receiver, and earned our-selves a reprimand. However, a couple of days later we heard that an enemy freighter had struck a mine and blown up in Brest harbour approach — to this day we always claim it as "Ours" ...

'1 January 1943
Aircraft "B"
Target: Bizerte, Tunisia (aiming point Bizerte docks/oil plants)
Bomb load: One 4,000lb Cookie

'Airborne from Blida 0229. Set course for Maison Blanche beacon, then time-run to turning point 30 miles off coast. Turned on course for Bizerte, checked position with back-bearing. Climbed to 6,000ft for minimum Cookie-height, and flying in cloud. Radio nav aids very poor so rely on dead reckoning. Through small break in cloud rear gunner reports surf below and we are crossing coast and drifting inland. Winds obviously strengthened from north and we are close to Philippeville. Much turbulence. Atlas mountain range only 20 miles inland. Change course to port and climb rapidly to try to break cloud for a star shot. Reached 13,000ft and still in cloud. Aircraft beginning to ice up rapidly. Position serious, cannot climb above cloud, weight of ice too much and airspeed falling off. Target only 20 miles to star-board. Decide on shallow descent to target area. Searchlights ahead through cloud. Aircraft vibrating badly and flying speed just above stalling. Select dropping position centre of searchlight ring and release bomb. With lightened load aircraft is climbed another 1,000ft and we break cloud at 14,000ft. Ice crystallises and breaks up, great chunks being flung off the props. We get a good astro fix and set course for home maintaining height. Home on to Maison Blanche beacon, then descend rapidly through cloud, icing up again. Cloud base has descended to 1,500ft and warmer air breaks up the icing. With a sigh of relief we cross coast and fly up the valley on the Blida beacon. Duration, six hours, 15mins.'

Tom Browne completed nearly 18 months of training for air crew duties

Below: Blida, viewed from the air on 9 February 1943. *N. L. Child*

Above: Fiume 'get's it' from a
104 Sqn Wimpy on
15 February 1945, viewed
from 15,000ft.

Left: Bizerta under attack by a
142 Sqn Wimpy, early 1943,
seen from 10,000ft.
N. L. Child

Above right: Trieste comes
under the bombsight of a 104
Sqn Wimpy on 17 February
1945, seen from 14,400ft.

as a pilot before reaching his first operational unit, to fly Wimpys against Germany. Finally having his name included in the night's battle order, he was understandably nervous, excited, yet fearful prior to the sortie:

'I was to go along for this first ride as second dickey, but it was to be my first proper operation against the enemy, and my breakfast kept threatening to bale out right from my first sight of my name on the board, right up until take-off. Veterans had reassured me that once I was airborne I'd be OK, but frankly I couldn't believe them. Came our turn to get the green from the runway controller and we started rolling — and I quickly realised that all that advice had been correct. I felt calm for the first time all day, and was really too damned busy trying to watch every item my hardbitten skipper attended to to be bothered with the butterflies doing aerobatics in my gut. Take-off was dead smooth — the skipper was a Geordie flight sergeant whose battered features suggested that he ate iron filings for dessert, but he had an oily DFM ribbon under his

wings — and we climbed away. The outward trip was uneventful (as far as I could see) and I remember being very thrilled privately when the nav announced ''Enemy coast coming up, skip''. Our target was Berlin — the ''Big City'' as the experienced crews called it — and we were just one of 14 Wimpys from our unit on this operation.

'As we approached the target area I could see fires, explosions and rising thick smoke clouds up ahead caused, presumably, by the first arrivals, while the sky seemed thick with flak bursts and writhing, twisting searchlights. To me it still seemed totally unreal, more like a Hollywood film or one of these bloody awful British moral-boosting war films they kept feeding the British public with at that time. We settled into our approach run-up for bombing and soon plunged in to the holocaust over the city suburbs. The Wimpy kept jumping about as near-miss flak bursts shoved her around in the sky, and I could hear occasional rattles and popping noises which (I realised later) were shell splinters lacing the fabric covering. We bombed OK and Geordie immediately banked hard and climbed at full boost to get out of the dangerous area. We almost made it too, but just as we were beginning to breathe a bit more freely, the rear gunner suddenly yelled, "Fighter! Fighter! Coming in fast behind!" Geordie swiftly flung the Wimpy into a quick dive, then banked hard to port, but not before that Jerry fighter had got one good burst into us.

'Cannon shells and bullets ripped right along the fuselage side, tearing fabric and ricochetting around off the geodetic framework. Straightening out again, we seemed to have lost the Jerry, so Geordie took stock of his crew. All reported OK, with no injuries, but the nav went up into the astro dome to check externally and told him that some shells had hit the port engine nacelle, and that it looked like some oil was trailing back over the wing. This was confirmed when the fuel gauges were checked — oil was slowly but steadily being lost. Temperature seemed reasonable for the moment, so Geordie decided to press on, keeping a watchful eye on the temperature reading for the engine. We flew fairly straight and level without attempting

to gain height until we were nearing the enemy coast again, and the damaged engine then decided it had had enough and started to overheat rapidly — it was obviously starved of oil. Geordie swore colourfully, feathered the prop, and told us to stand by in case he needed to bale us all out.

'We crawled over the coastline, still hoping to reach England but losing height all the time despite everything Geordie could do to keep the old girl going. The Wimpy continued its erratic course homewards while we all chewed our fingernails down to the elbow, and Geordie and I fought like hell to keep her nose pointed in the right direction on just one good engine. Our efforts were in vain — we'd have to ditch. The Wop sent off a fix and appropriate Mayday, then clamped down his Morse key before getting himself set — as we all were — for the sea landing. Geordie flattened the Wimpy out as we reached sea level, then tried to hold her off as long as possible. The first impact sounded like a corrugated sheet tearing off my garden shed roof in a high wind — the water coolly ripped out the belly of our aircraft in one go — we rose slightly

Left: W5359, QT-B of 142 Sqn at Binbrook in December 1940. *via R. Bonser*

Above: Sqn Ldr W. A. Smith in the cockpit of a 22 OTU Wellington at Wellesbourne Mountford, mid-1942. He was destined to be killed on 2 July 1943 in Short Stirling BK724 of 7 Sqn, during his second tour of operations. *R. Smith*

from the impact — then went down for good. The impact this time felt like hitting a brick wall, and I was flung forward, bashing my face on the structure hard. I passed out.

'The next thing I knew I was up to my ears in sea water with someone's arms under mine, supporting me. I couldn't see a damned thing, but after all it was still night-time. Several hands were then grabbing various parts of me or my suit and I felt myself being dragged over the rubbery side of a dinghy. My head felt as if it had been split down the middle, and I was far from fully compos mentis as yet, so I just lay where I'd been put; thankful vaguely to be out of the sea. I must have dozed off because when I next opened my eyes it was dawn, and I was no longer in a dinghy but lying on the deck of an ASR speedboat. I couldn't see anything out of my left eye, while my right eye was obviously puffed up because the lids were only just open. I put my hand to my head but only felt a wadge of cloth (it was a

field dressing roughly applied over the left eye). With some difficulty I looked around me — the rest of the crew were all there, thank God; all lying around, soaked to the skin, but very much alive. Geordie was the first to speak to me, asking how I felt. "Pretty bloody" was all I could mumble. His battered face had a couple of deep gashes now added to his laugh lines, as he had jokingly referred to his facial creases, but he seemed OK.

'I learned later that we'd been picked up fairly quickly by the ASR mercy angel, who happened to be on patrol not too far from our crash, looking for another Wimpy crew. (They never found them, by the way — poor sods). I went straight into the local civvy hospital when we landed, where I finally was told that I'd lost my left eye. Naturally, it meant no more flying for me — all that training for just one flip in anger. So now when anyone asks me "What did you do in the war?", I answer, "I bombed Berlin in a Wimpy — and I almost made it back too" . . .'

Artwork

Right: Sqn Ldr Joe McCarthy of 424 Sqn RCAF at Kairouan, Tunisia on 28 September 1943.
Public Archives of Canada

Below: Kiwi Devil. Insigne on a 75(NZ) Sqn Wellington, May 1941. *Crown copyright*

Below right: Wimpy WS-Z of 9 Sqn, 1941. 'Zola' was the girlfriend of the hero Buck Ryan in a contemporary *Daily Mirror* cartoon strip.
T. Mason

120

Above: Wellington III, X3794 of 9 Sqn. From left: Plt Off L. J. Brown, Sgt J. H. Harrison, 'Pam' (MT driver WAAF), Plt Off Jim Cowan (skipper of 'Barbara-Mary'), Sgt J. A. Talbot, Sgt R. W. Brown. *L. J. Brown*

Above right: Crew and 'bomb-siphon' insigne of a 75(NZ) Sqn Wimpy, May 1941. *Crown copyright*

Right: Wellington 'art' on a 405 Sqn RCAF aircraft, on 3 April 1942 at Topcliffe, Yorkshire. The mascot was named 'Moonshine', and the 'B' in the bomb log stood for sorties to Berlin. *Public Archives of Canada*

121

Left: Appropriate insigne on a 214 Sqn ('Federated Malay States') Sqn.

Below left: Blues in the Nite — a 425 Sqn RCAF Wimpy, viewed with its crew at Kairouan/Zina, Tunisia on 31 August 1943. *Public Archives of Canada*

Below: Flt Lt Jack MacCormack, pointing to his Wellington's dice insigne and name 'Dummy Run'. 405 Sqn RCAF, Pocklington, 14 August 1941. *Public Archives of Canada*

Right: 'Maximum Effort' was the 'title' of this 149 Sqn Wellington in 1941. The cow was usually named 'The Ozard of Whiz', and the Wimpy had completed 14 ops at the time of this photo

Far right and below right: Wellington X9684, 'Y' of 37 Sqn and its laughing donkey insigne, January 1942. *S. A. Barrett*

Above: The Saint, viewed at Aqir, 1943

Left: Slow but Sure, a bomb-carrying turtle, adorned this Wimpy in the Middle East, October 1943. Note DFC ribbon included in the bomb log recording 46 completed ops by day and by night. *Public Archives of Canada*

Below: A 150 Sqn Wellington, JN-A, believed to be R1016 (?), in which General Jimmy Doolittle flew on a sortie on 17/18 May 1943. The cartoon figure is 'Captain Reilly-Ffoul' of *Daily Mirror* strip-cartoon fame. *IWM*

Above: Wimpy of 99 Sqn at Digri, India in 1942. The motto to the 'coat of arms' read, 'Illegitimo non carborundum. Up your pipe. Let's s-it on Jerry' . . . *W. Hooper*

Right: Flt Sgt Art Jackson, Flt Sgt B. H. Tremblay, and Flt Sgt Joe Ross with *Chat-an-ooga-Choo-Choo* of 425 Sqn RCAF at Kairouan, Tunisia on 12 August 1943.
Public Archives of Canada

Below: Wimpy with a Bengal tiger insigne in India, circa 1944 (?). *B. Philpott*

Left: V for Victory — Wellington of 12 Sqn (W5376), 1941-42. *P. Small*

Right: Popeye, Wellington 'Z-Zebra' at Marham in October 1940.

Left: Wing Cdr B. J. Roberts, OC 12 Sqn in late 1941 at Binbrook (3rd from right) and crew. The insigne on the Wimpy appears to be a stag. *P. Small*

Right: Panel from Wellington W5430 'R' of 12 Sqn, Binbrook, which crash-landed after a raid on Cologne, 30 July 1941. *P. Small*

Centre right: Flt Lt Baxter, crew, and Wellington *Toujours* of 12 Sqn, Binbrook, 1941. The cartoon behind the motto depicts a female riding a boomerang.

Below: Tail-piece. Wellington rear gunner and his personal insigne for any Luftwaffe fighter closing in from behind, 1941. *British Official*

Bibliography

Vickers aircraft since 1908; C. F. Andrews; Putnam, 1969

Vickers Wellington I & II; C. F. Andrews; Profile No 125

Book of the Wellington; Real Publications, 1943

Pilot's Notes for Wellington; Air Publications 1578C/K/L/M/N; HMSO

Famous bombers of Second World War; W. Green; Macdonald, 1959

Aircraft of the RAF from 1918; O. Thetford; Putnam, 1976

RAF Bomber Squadrons; P. J. R Moyes; Macdonald, 1964

RAF Bomber Command (2 Vols); Moyes/Goulding; Ian Allan, 1975-78

RCAF Squadrons & Aircraft; Kostenuk/Griffin; 1977

Wellington Special; A. Lumsden; Ian Allan, 1974

Coastal Command at War; C. Bowyer; Ian Allan, 1979

Aircraft versus Submarines; A. W. Price; Wm Kimber, 1973

Desert Air Force; R. Owen; Hutchinson, 1948

Middle East; HMSO, 1944

Destiny can Wait; PAF Association; Heinemann, 1949

Pictorial history of the Mediterranean Air War (3 Vols); C. F. Shores; Ian Allan, 1972-74

9 Squadron; T. Mason; Beaumont Aviation, 1965

12 Squadron; T. Mason, Private, 1960

XV Squadron; N. J. Robertson; Private, 1975

The Black Swan (103 Sqn history); S. Finn; Unpublished ms.

The Sky is our ocean (311 Sqn); B. Rijnhout/J. P. Rennison; 1980

The mystery of L7788; B. Rijnhout; De Walburg Press, 1979

We Find and Destroy (458 Sqn); P. Alexander; 458 Sqn Council, 1959

In full flight; A. Spooner; Macdonald 1965

Pathfinder Cranswick; M. Cumming; Wm Kimber, 1962

Red Sky at Night; J. Capka; A. Blond, 1958

The Restless Sky; AVM C. E. Kay; Harrap, 1964

Popeye Lucas; F. J. Lucas; Reed, 1968

Acknowledgements

The following ex-Wellington crews, air and ground, provided the virtual 'spine' of this book. I owe each a debt of gratitude for invaluable and generous help, and can only hope they approve:

M. A. Alvis; J. Armstrong; F. L. Arrowsmith; E. A. Barclay; S. A. Barrett; D. Bolesworth; J. Bowles; P. Brewster; A. K. Brown; T. A. Browne, BEM; A. Butler; L. Cawley; G. S. W. Challen; N. L. Child; R. D. Cooling; A. Cullingworth; N. Didwell; E. R. Durrant; D. A Fraser; J. R. Gardner; W. Gilroy, DFM; Group Captain J.R. Goodman, DFC, AFC; L. Hallam; R. A. Hammersley, DFM; A. Hands; A. J. B. Harding; R. Harrington, DFC; R. R. Hartley; F. Hawkins; A. Hendrie; C. Hughes, DFC; R. Humphries; A. E. Husk; Wing Commander E. G. Jones; L. H. Jordan; J. O. Lancaster, DFC; C. Lofthouse; Group Captain E. H. Lynch-Blosse, OBE; R. S. McGill; N. E. McIntyre; Group Captain N. E. Montague-Smith, DL; J. M. Morvell; J. H. F. Murphy; P. Payne; D. W. Pinches; F. N. Plum; D. Porter; P. G. Powell; J. Price; A. Ramsay; L. Read; E. A. Sanders, DFC; Group Captain M. J. A. Shaw, DSO; A. Showell; J. Skinner; R. Slater; S. J. Sterrett; W. R. Stevenson, DFM; E. M. Summers; R. G. Thackeray, DRM; W. Tidy; A. Wahlroth, BA, OD; Wing Commander K. H. Wallis, C Eng, FRAeS, FRSA; P. S. F. Walmsley, DFC; J. Ware, DFM; R. W. Watson; K. Westrope; D. M. White; W. E. Wilkinson; G. F. Wilson; R. Wratten.